Whan that Aprille
For the curious: an exploration of the South Downs Way in Hampshire

Whan that Aprille

First Edition

ISBN 978-0-9928041-9-0

First published in Great Britain by Heather Lacey
using the services of REDBAK Publishing.

REDBAK Publishing
United Kingdom

Printed in United Kingdom

Cover Design by
Think Tank inc Design
thinktankincdesign.com

About the Author

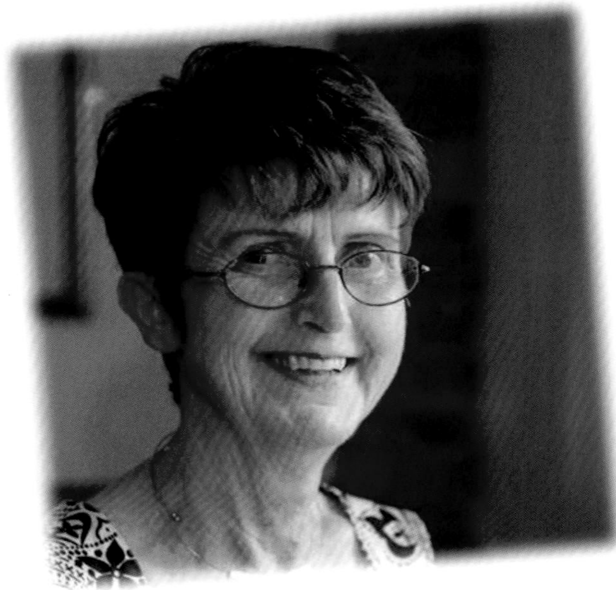

Born and bred in the London suburbs, Heather's great escape in her youth was those wonderful green London Country Buses, enabling her to roam in fields of North West Kent.

Leaving school at fifteen, she swore never to go into a school again. However, useless at keeping promises to herself, following higher education she spent over thirty years enjoying teaching English to teenagers in Kent. Eventually, having despaired of ticking boxes rather than broadening the knowledge, understanding and interest of the subject for her students, she almost managed to escape, becoming a supply teacher (or 'Super-Teacher' as she prefers to call it).

With the greater freedom she now has, Heather has enjoyed devoting her time to her many and varied hobbies, including walking.

Her dalliance with the South Downs Way was spoiled by two things: terrible weather and the lack of a book about the area which would satiate her curiosity. Unable to do anything about the weather, she decided to find out curious and interesting things about the people, places and history either side of the South Downs Way.

By the time she reached the Hampshire/Sussex border, she'd found enough to fill a book.

With thanks to...

Steve Cannings and Dave Axton who have given up many weekends to produce some wonderful pictures, and to others who have donated images, including Ruth Yeoman, Sue Sutton, Chris Capel, The Revd. Gordon Plumb, Simon Downs from the Hampshire Astronomical Group, and Freya Fradenburgh. Thanks also to The Mary Rose Trust, the Bayeux Museum, Winchester Science Centre, Holden Farm, Butser Ancient Farm and The MCC and Nick Browne for their help and provision of photographs.

In Winchester, I'd like to thank the staff at the Hampshire Record Office, as well as the guides at the Cathedral, and also Suzanne Foster at Winchester College. The staff at Portsmouth Historic Dockyard also need a mention, as does Peter Corrigan from the William Morris Gallery in Walthamstow for help with the identification of the window at Meonstoke. Terena Plowright is to be thanked for her help with sheep, as is Elaina Whittaker-Slark at the South Downs Way National Park Authority. The help and encouragement from the Sustainability Centre is also greatly appreciated.

In particular, I'd like to thank the people of Hampshire who have generously shared their time and knowledge, as well as having some wonderful events including cakes and flowers. Especial thanks are owed to the vicars and church wardens who have emailed me useful information, guided me around their churches and answered numerous questions. I must not forget the landlords who have welcomed me into their pubs, and in particular the Quizzers at the Isaac Walton for their welcome and enthusiasm.

The keen gardeners of the National Gardens Scheme – Victoria Wakefield, Julian Blackwell and Jenny Privett – are also owed thanks, as is the Wheely Down Forge and the West Meon Pottery.

Friends, including Terry and Sharon Everett and David Straker must also be thanked.

I am highly indebted to Doug Jones at Buriton, Michael Blakstad from the East Meon History Group, Tim King from Droxford for ongoing information and advice, Ron Stone for his knowledge of the Meon Valley Railway, and especially to George Watkinson at the St Cross Almshouse in Winchester for his knowledge, enthusiasm and friendship.

And finally, thanks to Miles Allen for his guidance and hard work in dragging me though the processes needed to produce this book.

Picture Credits

Thanks to all those who have donated pictures, many of which are acknowledged within the book. However, many more are listed here.

vi	*Time*	*© Steve Cannings*
vii	*Garden: East Meon Festival*	*© Steve Cannings*
viii	*Landscape*	*© Steve Cannings*
ix	*Milking Time (i)*	*© Steve Cannings*
ix	*Milking Time (ii)*	*© Steve Cannings*
x	*Heat and Energy*	*© Charles Normandale*
xi	*Gate: Four Seasons*	*at the Wheely Down*
xi	*Detail: Silver Shoon*	*Forge.*
xii	*Tree*	*© Steve Cannings*
xiii	*Flying*	*© Steve Cannings*

198	Butterflies	© Sue Sutton
199	Herdwick at Old Winchester Hill	© Steve Cannings
200	Time out at Old Winchester Hill	© Steve Cannings
202	Accommodation	© various contributors
203	Fishing	© Steve Cannings
204	Ewe and lambs	© Steve Cannings
205	Charity walk along the SDW	© Steve Cannings
206	Landscape: to the West	© Steve Cannings
209	The George Inn	© Steve Cannings
211	The Domesday Village	© With special permission from the town of Bayeux

213	Beautiful craftsmanship Amens Plenty	2 x © Steve Cannings
215	Courthouse gateway	© Steve Cannings
226	Towards the Downs	© Steve Cannings
228	The Natural Burial Ground	2 x © Steve Cannings
229	Taking a break Wetherdown Lodge	1. © Steve Cannings 2. Thanks to the Sustainablity Centre
230	Family time	© Steve Cannings

Many of the pictures uncredited within the book itself are listed here and their copyright acknowledged. If you would like a mounted copy of any of these pictures please contact Dave Axton or Steve Cannings directly at:

imagedax@gmail.com (for Dave)

or

mistersteeb@hotmail.com (for Steve)

Other uncredited pictures are snaps I took as I wandered around the county

Contents

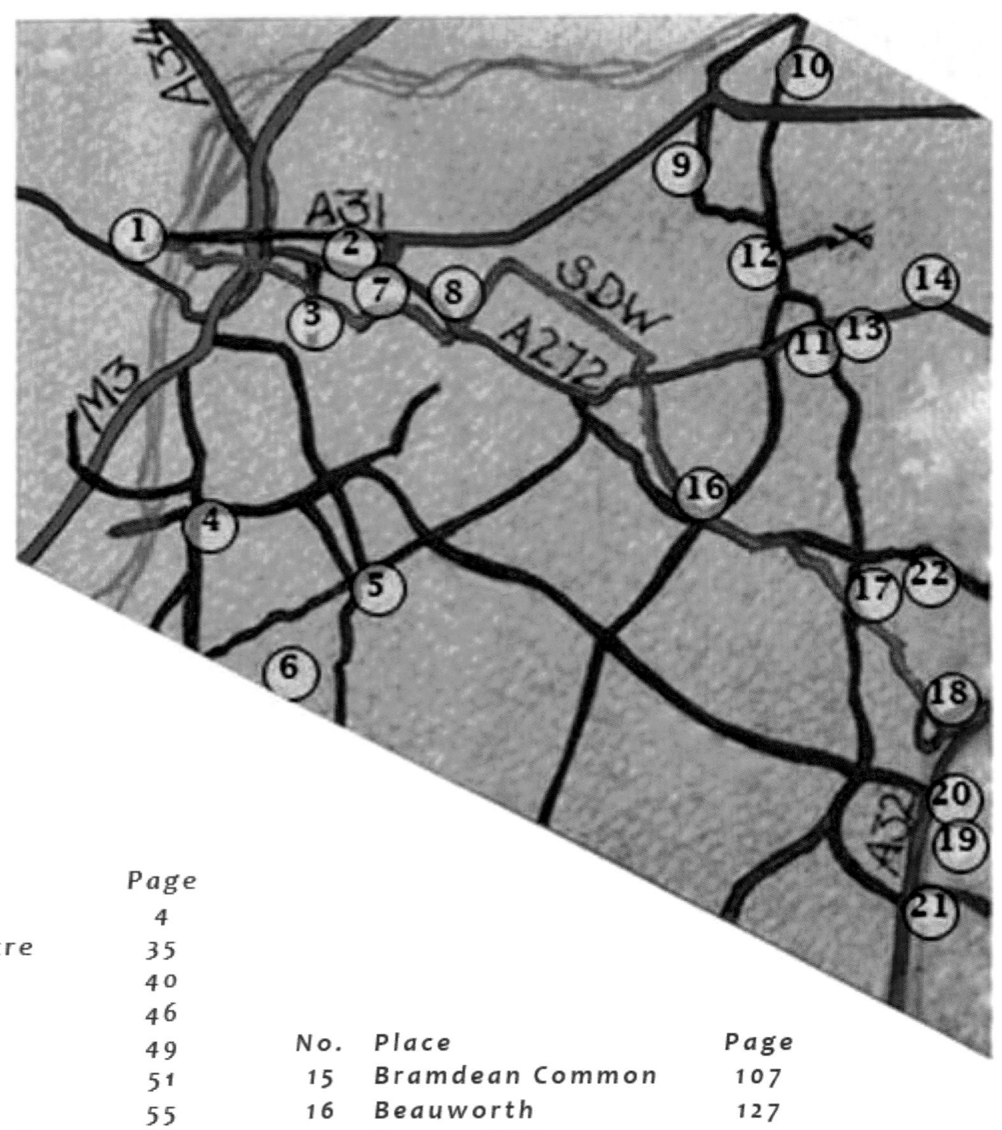

What You'll Find Where

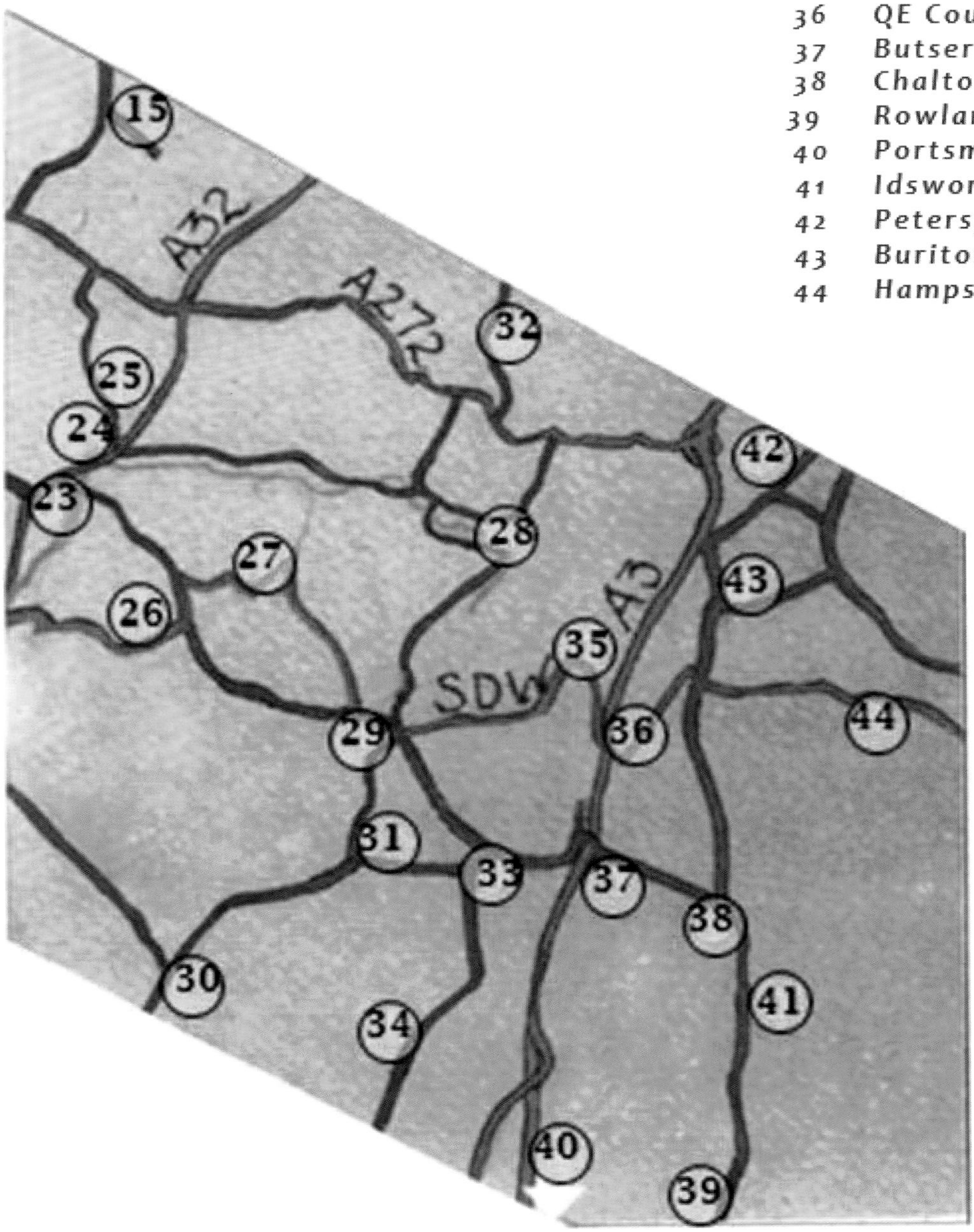

15
A32
A272
32
25
24
42
23
28
27
43
A3
26
35
SDW
29
36
44
31
33
37
38
30
41
34
40
39

Prologue

When April with his showers sweet with fruit
The drought of March has pierced unto the root

As an avid laid-back walker, I like to try new places, and this time I set my sights on the South Downs Way. Shopping for a guide, I only found the usual books. You know the sort: the 'Turn right at the third horse on the left' variety. They require knowledge and practise with map and compass work which, to the unskilled, is a world of mystery to me and, I'm sure, puts off many others, especially after getting lost a few times. Those are the books that get put into the "I'll read it later" pile.

Some fellow walkers were carrying copies of the same tome as me, as they too were among this season's early starters from Winchester, the former capital city of England. Others were guided by a long thin map focusing on the route, but uncluttered by a myriad of other guiding features.

Somewhere in their rucksacks, many – I suspect – also had their OS Maps and compasses!

Perusing the books available at Stanford's in Covent Garden – over coffee and cake – I chose the one where I thought I could follow the route most easily.

So, clutching the trusty guide, I made my way from Winchester for the first thirty miles of The South Downs Way, through East Hampshire and into West Sussex. April may seem a little early in the walking season, but if Chaucer's pilgrims could make their way from London to Canterbury in this month, then I could make my way from another starting point for pilgrims, who had made their journey hoping for benefice from the spirit of Saint Thomas.

Countryside cottage in Tichborne

Although at times the weather made it impossible to see any views from the pathway, I was sure that there were villages and towns either side of me as I roamed, and sometimes – looking down into a valley or peering over a hedge – I could actually see that they really did exist. The problem was that, being an inquisitive person, I wanted to know more about these places: history, personalities, buildings, events, phenomena, curiosities… anything interesting!

If I could be nosy, then I had the feeling that other travellers might be intrigued too. Yes, there are many cottages and villages which match the 'chocolate box' image, but up the winding streets there had to be more!

So, it occurred to me that someone had to do the donkey work. And that, perhaps, I should be the one to do it.

After my trusty route-guide became a soggy mass, following an April shower, with pages stuck together, unable to be separated for some days, I considered that, as well as a book, an 'app' would be a good idea as this was likely to tolerate moistness more readily. It would also be lighter to carry than a book and less cumbersome than turning pages in a storm. However, as work progressed – getting bigger and bigger – I realised that the batteries would go flat far too soon! Books, on the other hand, are *best to curl up with, on the sofa, with a large mug of hot chocolate!*

Hampshire landscape

Winchester

Of course, journeying from the Western end of the walk, my starting point was Winchester, and I definitely recommend that some time is spent exploring this city before moving towards Eastbourne!

The Eclipse, The Square

Beers and Spirits

There are many pubs in Winchester, and any one of them can make an excellent starting point.

One of them is The Eclipse, just around the corner from the cathedral. Although the building is from the latter part of Henry VIII's reign, it is a lady from over a hundred years after this who is still talked about.

Lady Alicia Lisle

The ghost of Lady Alicia Lisle of Moyles Court, Ellingham in Hampshire, is said to haunt its environs! "Hanging" Judge Jeffries condemned the lady to death for giving shelter to rebels during the Monmouth Rebellion of the 1680s.

Her final hours before her beheading on the 2nd September, 1685 were spent in an upstairs room at The Eclipse. A platform was erected opposite the inn and she walked directly from an upper window to her execution. Since that time, the ghost of the Lady in Grey has often been seen, or her footsteps heard.

In fact, there appear to be more ghosts in the area than in your average town. One website (www.paranormaldatabase.com/hotspots/winchester.php) lists fourteen, but there are even more spectral visits in the area to be found on other sites.

Mediaeval Metropolis?

Winchester's propensity to be weighed down by such vaporous visions can be justified by the city's long and meritorious role in the history of England. For many centuries Winchester was the capital city of England: it was the seat of kings, the centre of political life, a prize in war, and a commercial hub. Never mind the Arthurian connections, its history is enough to fill books galore. There are so many places to visit; here I can only skim over some of the highlights that may justify a visit. Hopefully, like me, your appetite will be whetted and you will be tempted to linger a while.

The Headmaster's house at The Pilgrims' School

The Tourist Information Centre has maps for the area and can suggest places connected with its political, religious, or military past with a host of other places that may pique your particular interests.

In Roman times it was the fifth largest city in England, and its pre-eminence continued for many centuries. In the Ninth Century, it was King Alfred's capital city.

William the Conqueror, to make sure that everyone knew he was king, had two coronations: one in London and the second in Winchester. It is more than likely that – two decades later – he then chose the local monks to investigate and write the Domesday Book: a census of everything and everyone in England. I have been told Winchester appears to have been omitted (perhaps because the monks said "Oh, we know that one, so we'll leave it 'til later!"). Certainly, the various surveys were collated in Winchester.

William the Conqueror had three surviving sons: Robert – who stayed in Normandy – William Rufus and Henry. When William Rufus died in 1100, it was to Winchester that his younger brother Henry rode to secure the crown of England and – more importantly – the royal treasure!

Mediaeval kings were as likely to be ruling from Winchester as they were from London. It was only after things started to go downhill for the Royalists in the English Civil War that Winchester's status declined.

King Alfred still looks over Winchester today

It was not just politically that Winchester has been noted in the annals of history. For example, literature has its call upon the city: Jane Austen spent her final weeks in the city.

Also, Anthony Trollope went to the college and also based the fictional Barchester upon his time here, and John Keats wrote 'Ode to Autumn' while here.

The house next to Winchester College where Jane Austen spent her final weeks

Jane Austen's memorial in the Cathedral

Ringin' your bell

Winchester Cathedral; New Vaudeville Band, 1966

As the South Downs Way begins close by Winchester Cathedral, you may find it fitting to find out more about this famous landmark. The Cathedral goes back to the early Christians in England, in the 7th Century. Members of the Saxon royal family were buried here.

Towards the West Door of the Cathedral

As I write, the skeletons of five kings and one queen are being sorted out, as at some time in their history they have all been mixed up!

This may well have happened when the Parliamentarians, during the Civil War, used the bones as clubs to smash the stained glass and some of the statues around the building.

The good news is that all the shards of glass were gathered up and were arranged as a collage for the West Window. What a smashing time they all must have had!

You Can't Make an Omelette Without...

15th July . . . Dear Diary . . . Today is the first day of my walking holiday. It rained!

Back to those Anglo-Saxon times, and perhaps the most famous person we remember with connections to Winchester Cathedral is Saint Swithun. He's the one with the 'day' on 15th July.

Legend has it that should it rain on that day, it will continue to do so for the next forty days.

The egg shell design on Saint Swithun's shrine

However, it wasn't for his meteorological skills that he was made a saint. He also performed miracles. But it's not for anyone he healed that he was headline news: it was for eggs. A basket of eggs was dropped when a short-sighted monk bumped into a farmer's wife. Saint Swithun remedied the situation by making the eggs whole again. That's why the columns of his shrine have brass eggshells incorporated in them, not raindrops! Mind you, this shrine is not the original: that is long gone!

Saint Swithun's ability to control the weather only came about when his body was moved in 972 AD from its location in the graveyard to its more prestigious spot inside the old Saxon minster, when he seems to have started sulking and punishing us all with soggy summers! Sometime in the last thousand years or so we've lost track of him altogether. Perhaps that accounts for Global Warming!

Smite be Fun!

Nevertheless, it is not just St Swithun who was rather vengeful: God himself seems to have got involved over the issue of William Rufus, King of England, son of William the Conqueror.

Not the most popular monarch, he ruled for thirteen years, his reign being brought to its end in 1100, in The New Forest, where he was 'accidentally' shot with an arrow by one of his soldiers while out hunting.

His remains were taken to Winchester and placed in the Choir of the newly built Cathedral. God, however, was so outraged by this desecration, in 1107 He smote the Cathedral's tower so it collapsed. A good bit of smiting is a lovely way to release tension, don't you find? Well, the body was removed and, as the tomb was in a very desirable location, it was a shame to waste it.

So a few centuries later, the remains of a former bishop, Henry of Blois, (Bishop, Lord Chancellor of England, brother to King Stephen), were dug up from Cluny in France and given the prime location in Winchester.

Being the King's brother was probably a good way to further anyone's career. And the Bishopric of Winchester was definitely a 'plum job': it was the second-richest diocese in Europe and, what with all the bonuses of fines, quit rents (payments to avoid doing things like military service) and other payments from over sixty manors in the South of England, it must have been a very comfortable job.

And the location! Whereas 'the office' for most of us is a boxy-looking room, the Bishop of Winchester enjoyed the longest nave in Europe in mediaeval times, at 554 feet – even Milan could only boast a mere 520 feet! Once the Renaissance was under way, Winchester was beaten by St Peter's in Rome at 614 feet, but the old St Peter's was a pretty insignificant 340 feet.

So all-in-all, being Bishop of Winchester – as many a lucky chap knew – was a humdinger of a job to have!

Neither King Stephen himself nor William Rufus did particularly well in the popularity stakes, but at least they did add to Winchester Cathedral's history.

Another not-so-popular monarch was married in Winchester Cathedral. Queen Mary, daughter of Henry VIII, married King Phillip II of Spain in July 1554. The marriage followed rioting by her people, who were dismayed at the Catholic alliance. The happy couple had met only two days before the wedding and, much to the delight of her subjects, Phillip did not hang around in England very often after that date.

The Cathedral's impressive length

Bishop Stephen Gardiner officiated as, thanks to Mary's Catholic faith, he was in one of his 'up' periods. His fortunes ebbed and flowed with the changing religious tides of

Tudor England. Following his death, he was buried in the Cathedral, where his effigy can still be seen.

Mary's reign was short-lived anyway: she died in 1558. Phillip was not there at the time and when he did hear of her death, he wrote in a letter: "I felt reasonable regret for her death. I shall miss her..."

Shortly afterwards, he felt the need for a new bride and suggested an alliance with Queen Elizabeth, Mary's sister!

Winchester today is a thriving community

As well as many popular shops, the street market has everything from fruit and fashion, through hummus and household goods to vegetables and veal!

Damp Nuisance!

Even though the remains of many famous people (including the 17th-century angler Izaak Walton and the writer Jane Austen) have been interred at Winchester, some people may not regard it at the most comfortable place to hang out until judgement day, as it is likely to be rather damp.

The eastern end of the cathedral was built on rather soggy ground in Mediaeval times, and by the early 20th century the foundations had bitten the dust (well, bitten the sludge, if you are pedantic).

Urgent underpinning was required, but the water-table was so high the foundations were under water. Consequently, a deep-sea diver was required!

So, for six years from 1906, William Walker – who had the right credentials – whilst wearing one of those large, old-fashioned diving suits, spent six hours a day wading into the water to lay sacks of cement beneath the foundations. What a thing to be able to put on your CV!

Towards the choir stalls

This guy obviously had a lot of energy to complete such a task, particularly as he and his wife had several children during this time!

He died, in 1919, during the Spanish Flu epidemic.

There is a memorial to 'Diver Bill' in the Cathedral. As people have looked at the sculpture of the man himself, they have been deceived! The original sculptor, when looking at a photograph, made a mistake and used the features of Bill's boss, Sir Francis Fox! Ah: "fame (as the American poet, Emily Dickinson said) is a fickle food upon a shifting plate."

Fortunately, the memorial has been replaced by a new figure, which I understand is the real McCoy! There is another sculpture of Bill in a nook by the visitors' centre.

William Walker's labours were given royal acknowledgement, as he was awarded the MVO (Member of the Victorian Order), a gift from the Monarch, by King George the Fifth.

Although stable, the waters still rise up inside the Cathedral these days.

Diver Bill's monument, standing quietly in the courtyard

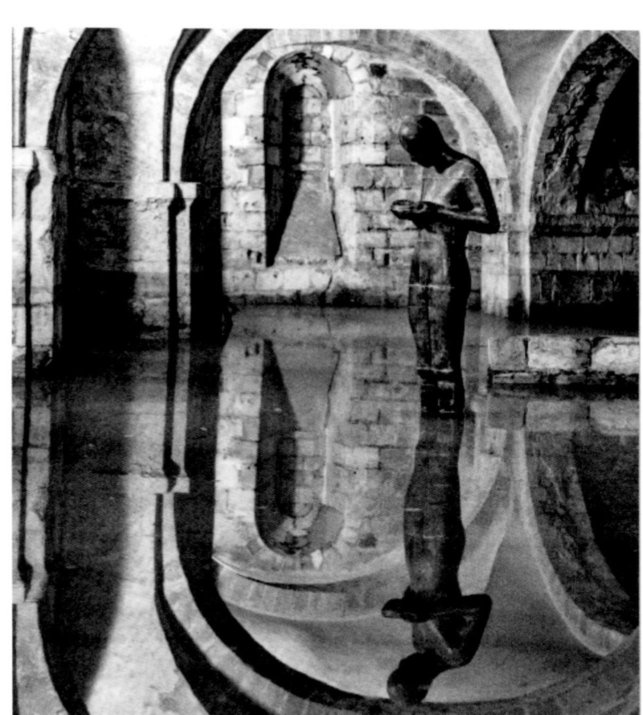

Sound II by Antony Gormley

A visit to the crypt reveals a statue by Antony Gormley that seems to float on a shimmering pool of water. In times of flooding, the figure seems to be not wading, but drowning! Although, looking at the chap, he appears to be texting someone.

A lot of the gravestones in the floor of the Cathedral have the letters HSE engraved upon them, which stands for the Latin 'Hic Sepultus (or Situs) Est' which means 'Here Lies'. Considering the sogginess of the area, perhaps it really stands for Health and Safety Executive!

A grave example of HSE engraving

As there are tours around the Cathedral, you can take advantage of the guides' knowledge or stroll around by yourself while you are in the area.

Then, the school-boy with his satchel and shining morning face

Jaques: As You Like It; Wm. Shakespeare

Another place worth a visit is the college. Winchester College was founded in the Middle Ages by William of Wykeham – a local lad made good and a former bishop of the Cathedral – and has been the alma mater of many notable figures over the generations from English politics, the military, and society, including Lord Alfred Douglas (Oscar Wilde's Bosie), Labour Party leader Hugh Gaitskell and the comic actor and panellist Tim Brooke-Taylor.

Like most of our ancient public schools, it was initially a charitable foundation, to provide an education for poor boys. Although there are bursaries, most of the pupils these days pay fees in excess of what most of us earn in a year!

Winchester College provided scholarship places for seventy pupils and there are still scholars in College Hall. So, in the twenty-first century eighteen percent of pupils receive a bursary, all means tested, fulfilling the wishes of its founder, William Wykeham, who also established New College at Oxford.

As you travel towards the East over the coming days, you will pass nearby the village of Wickham, his birthplace. Despite his humble roots, through patronage he gained an education which enabled him not only to rise to be Bishop of Winchester, but also to become Chancellor of England during the reigns of both Edward III and Richard II.

The official motto for the school is "Manners maykth Man", which I think should be adopted by motorists up and down the country! Traditionally, the school has a second motto: "Learn, leave or be beaten", meaning that if you fail to learn or take up a respectable career you will be a loser in life!

Guided tours are also available at the college if you want to know more. I found it very interesting. Details can be found at www.winchestercollege.org/guided-tours.

Taken to the Cleaners

The chapel windows are particularly beautiful, with their colourful stained glass. In 1821 the college fellows were dismayed by the poor condition of the mediaeval windows, which were so caked in grime that very little light would permeate through. Thus it was that the glass was carefully removed and sent for cleaning to some highly recommended restorers in Shrewsbury.

When they were returned, the vivid colours so delighted the masters of the college, with luscious lilacs, brilliant blues, and gorgeous greens, they sent their remaining glass to be renovated too.

This must have dismayed the craftsmen in Shropshire, but the work was completed to the same high standard. For almost century the stunning glass delighted those at the college and its visitors.

However, an eagle-eyed observer might focus on God sitting astride the Globe at the top. Visible for all to see is Australia! You might wonder: how did mediaeval glass-workers know about the Antipodes so long before Captain Cook?

The Victorian replacement window

The restored Mediaeval window

(Copyright, Revd Gordon Plumb, used by permission of Winchester College)

Investigation showed that even the best cleaning methods in pre-Victorian times could not produce a satisfactory result on the filthy fragments. So, the craftsmen in the Midlands painstakingly reproduced the windows and sent brand-new ones back to the college in the latest nineteenth-century colours. Although a few of the senior staff wised up pretty quickly, the majority of folks were kept in the dark for many years.

To recoup their losses, the partially cleaned originals were sold by the restoration company to delighted owners of stately homes up and down the country.

By the start of the First World War, the then bursar was on the case, wondering if it was possible to track down the ancient glass and bring it home. But it took until after the Second World War to reclaim most of it.

With the help of Lord Kenneth Clarke, of 'Civilization' fame, in tracking down those originals, the journey home was facilitated. Much of the glass was bought back by the college and now forms a window in the side-chapel.

Even with modern cleaning methods, it has not been a case of bang and the grime is gone, but by grinding away at the grubby surface, some of the sparkle has been restored.

However, the final piece is there, but it is on loan from the Victoria and Albert Museum, which is not allowed to sell any of its exhibits

Winchester Castle

Unfortunately, the castle does not exist anymore! But do not be down-hearted as the Great Hall does remain.

The castle had a prominent role in the Middle Ages, not only as a centre of rule for the whole country, but as a stronghold for various factions in civil wars and other disputes.

For example, it was held by both Stephen and Matilda at different times as they fought for the crown of England in the twelfth century.

In the later Civil War it was used by the Royalists and, upon their defeat, by Oliver Cromwell. He was very cavalier with the building: he knocked it down!

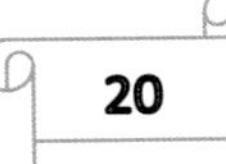

Not only was the castle used to keep people out, it was also used to keep people in. King Henry II, challenged by his strong-willed wife – Eleanor of Aquitaine – and their sons, imprisoned his spouse within its walls.

Castles can often claim to have had prisoners, but Winchester Castle's Great Hall (the only bit to remain) was also used as a place of justice, right up to modern times. Most famously over the years, Sir Walter Raleigh was tried here, and in the 1970s IRA members were also tried here.

Exterior of the Great Hall

It was also here that Lady Alicia Lisle, who still has her presence in modern Winchester at The Eclipse, had her trial. Originally, her sentence was to be burnt at the stake but she was saved from such a gruesome end when it was commuted to hanging!

Murder Most Foul! *Hamlet; Wm. Shakespeare*

Winchester's Court heard a case in 1867 involving the most gruesome of murders, which has gone down in English history for lexicographical reasons rather than for it making legal history.

The perpetrator of the crime, a solicitor's clerk called Frederick Baker, had murdered an eight-year-old child some eighteen miles away, at Alton. The tragedy was made worse by the grotesque mutilation of the corpse, leaving the remains beyond recognition. The young man was found guilty and was hanged outside the County Prison on the morning of Christmas Eve, 1867.

The first notable point of this case was that this was one of the final public hangings in the country, viewed by five thousand spectators.

Subsequently, a chain of small events began, resulting in a second notable point.

Unsurprisingly, the press had made much of this horrendous case, raising it in the public's consciousness. So much so, sailors used the poor victim's name in jest to describe some of their rations. Tinned mutton was provided for their repast, but it was so mangled in the tins it was unrecognisable.

Thus it was that the sailors referred to the contents as 'Sweet Fanny Adams'. Through common usage, it began to mean 'nothing at all'. In time, Sweet Fanny Adams was contracted to Sweet FA, and since then it has degenerated into a euphemism for another impolite phrase!

My Knight in Shining Armour!

When people think of the Great Hall they generally think of the round table, King Arthur, chivalry and the good-old-bad-old days!

Now, we've all made sure that we get our fair share when it comes to dishes on the table in a restaurant, well the Great Hall has something that looks like the biggest 'Lazy-Susan' in the world!

Newly-weds leaving the Register Office in the old Law Court buildings

It's supposed to be King Arthur's Round Table, but was really made during the reign of King Edward I (doesn't carbon-dating spoil the romance of legend and history?), who was fanatical about all things Arthurian...knights, chivalry, round tables, rescuing damsels in distress...

Well, actually, no: the ladies had to wait a few hundred years for tournaments to get in on that act – and by then the tournaments had become more like rather violent church fetes!

King Edward's version was more to do with bravery, fighting the infidel and killing people. However, the romance of Geoffrey of Monmouth's King Arthur in his 'History of the Kings of Britain' was taking its hold on people's imagination and it is still with us today with Mills and Boon stories as well as teenage fiction! And rather like a band will re-release a good song, we shouldn't forget Thomas Mallory's 'Mort de Arthur' from 1485 (the year of the coronation of the first Tudor monarch), which is perhaps better known and was responsible for a re-flowering of the Arthurian myth in Tudor times.

The Order of the Garter was founded by Edward III in 1348, and is still the highest honour that can be awarded by the monarch. Its precursor was The Order of the Round Table, which was part of the mediaeval craze for all things Arthurian and its links to Winchester.

The Round Table

This Delicious Solitude

The Garden; Andrew Marvell

A doorway from The Great Hall leads into a beautiful spot: Queen Eleanor's Garden. Perhaps it should be Queen Eleanors' Garden, as there were quite a few queens called Eleanor in mediaeval times and this a tribute to two of them.

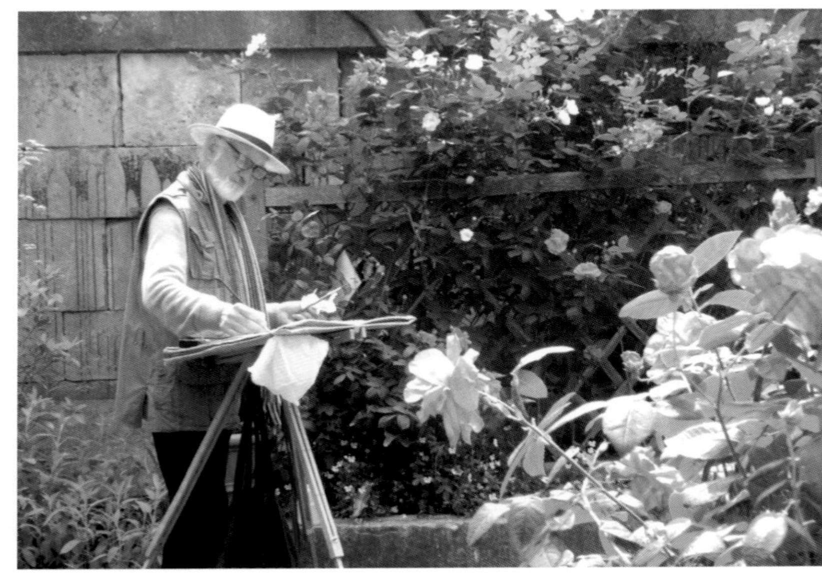

An artist's tranquil moment in the garden

King Henry III was the monarch responsible for the rebuilding of the castle in the middle of the thirteenth century, including the Great Hall which remains to this day.

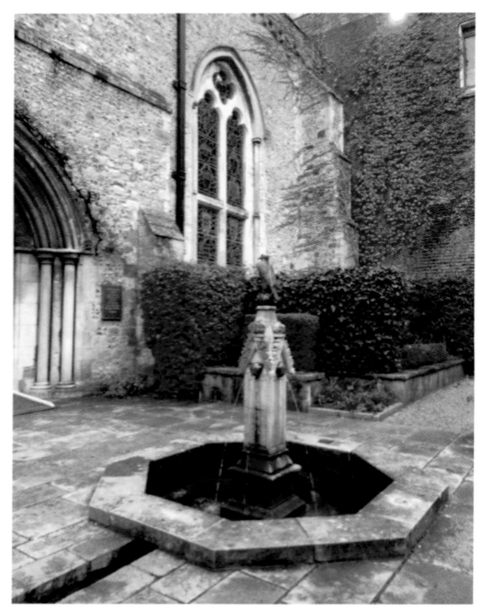

The fountain

He was married to an Eleanor: of Provence. His son, King Edward I, married an Eleanor too: she was Eleanor of Castile, the one remembered most for the crosses that marked her final journey to Westminster Abbey following her death in 1290, nearby to Lincoln.

Oh dear! A few friends looking at this have given me really puzzled looks as they don't know about those Eleanor Crosses! So, although it is rather a big diversion from Hampshire, perhaps I need to make a little excursion half way up the country to Lincolnshire!

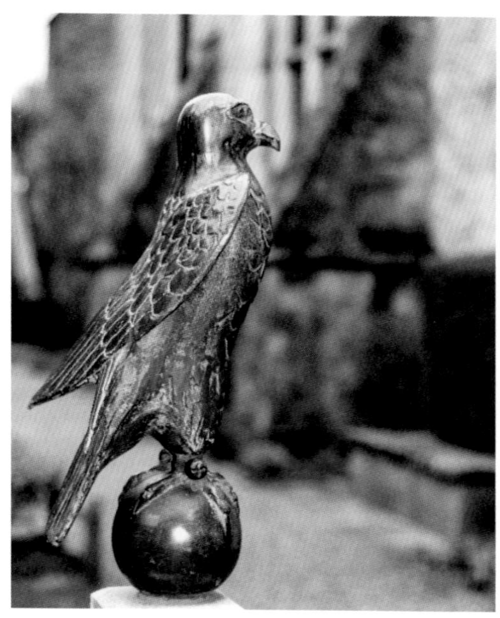
A detail on the fountain

From Lincoln, Queen Eleanor's body was carried to London, taking twelve days and, where it rested overnight, Edward had memorial crosses erected. Travelling via Stamford, Woburn, St Albans and Waltham Cross – among other places – its final stop on the journey to Westminster Abbey was Charing Cross. Only three of the original crosses remain, the best preserved at Geddington, although there are fragments of others, and a few have been reconstructed.

Perhaps the most well-known is Charing Cross, and sure enough: it stands there in all its glory on the forecourt of the railway station!

Ah! The first trouble is that this is a nineteenth-century reproduction – the Victorians always thought they could do Gothic better than the Gothics – the first cross having been destroyed during the Civil War in the seventeenth century. The second disappointment is that it was never in this location in the first place. It was on the South side of what is now Trafalgar Square!

After more than seven hundred years, I suppose it is not a surprise that so little evidence of the romantic memorials from a king to his queen still remain.

That Edward made this sentimental gesture towards his queen shows another side of the man better known as the Hammer of the Scots for his brutality to those in the North, and who was equally ruthless in his land-grabbing in both Wales and France.

Both of these Queen Eleanors were noted for their style and, what I suppose these days we'd call being fashionistas! Eleanor of Castile liked wall tapestries and carpets, making them fashionable. Outdoors, she was keen on garden design and she was influential in the planning of gardens in royal properties of the period, often including water features.

Sadly, this garden is not a left over relic from days-gone-by, but a modern interpretation. Despite that, after some hours of being a tourist around the city, it is a decidedly pleasant place to chill-out following the long walk up the hill! The design and planting do reflect how gardens were used in the past, although this was made as recently as the 1980s. Gardens were not only places to relax but also places to grow food and plants with medicinal qualities. Apart from the last, it does seem very much like the average garden these days!

The choice of planting here is based on what would have been in England at the time of these two queens. From Asparagus through to Wormwood, via Calendula and Tansy, there was plenty to choose from (no daffs or delphiniums then!)

I remember a time when I liked a red coat myself very well

Mrs Bennet; Pride and Prejudice; Jane Austen

Winchester's pre-eminent status through the middle ages meant that its castle had to be easily defendable in times of conflict. Its military connections, therefore, stretch back a long way. This history is celebrated in the five military museums that you will find in the city.

Situated where the castle once stood, proudly overlooking the town, the army barracks as they stand now were built in the early twentieth century. In the two and a half centuries between the destruction of the castle by Oliver Cromwell's troops, the site had been designated as a new palace by Charles II and later as army barracks. The site had been destined to be a new palace designed by Sir Christopher Wren for the newly restored monarchy after the Commonwealth.

Never finished, it was used to house prisoners of war following skirmishes with the French, the Spanish and the Dutch, as well as Americans from the War of Independence. In its next life it became army barracks and remained so for almost two centuries.

However, during that time, the remains of the palace were razed to the ground by fire in 1894. It was then reborn as a modern army base, in use up until 1986, when the army moved to a new barracks built outside Winchester. Now, this city-centre site is the location of a wealth of information on Britain's army, past and present.

With so many museums, if you are intending to visit, this can take some time, so do allow a big enough space in your schedule! Two of the museums – The Royal Hampshire Regiment and The Guardroom – are free. The other three (Horsepower, The Royal Green Jackets and the Gurkha ones) do charge for admission.

Although Lizzie Bennet's mother in 'Pride and Prejudice' reminisced about her youthful longings for a soldier in a red coat, it was not officers from Hampshire's own regiment that turned her head, as they have always worn the colour green!

The army parade ground as it is today

And if you've still got some time on your hands...

Winchester can lay claim to yet another castle. This time it is Wolvesey Castle. Again, only its ruins remain.

The ruins of Wolvesey Castle

It seems odd to have had a bishop living in a castle, but when you even outrank the Archbishop of Canterbury, and you are Chief Advisor to the King (Stephen), as well as – coincidentally – being the King's brother, you probably need something a little sturdier than your average semi-detached to live in. As Winchester Castle had seen better days by then by the time that Queen Mary married Phillip of Spain, Wolvesey Castle was used for the wedding breakfast following their nuptials.

Exploring the castle – a Norman archway

The Spanish had not been overawed by the English, especially the pallor of the Queen, but the dancing that took place afterwards, including that of Her Majesty, did impress! It's good to know that the footwork of the English on the dance floor is strictly impressive, even if our footwork on the pitch can vary.

God that feedeth the young ravens will take care of me also.

Barchester Chronicles; Anthony Trollope

You may also wish to visit the Hospital of St Cross, which can be found towards the South of Winchester, not far off the South Downs Way. No, it is not the A&E department of the local hospital, so I'm not suggesting that, having done the tourist-trail, you've collapsed with exhaustion!

The St Cross Almshouses

As hospital, hostel, hospitality are all similar words, it will not surprise you that this hospital, founded in the early 1130s, was a charitable establishment, an almshouse, originally for thirteen poor men.

In addition, '100 other poor persons' were given a daily meal. They were also allowed to take any leftovers with them, which meant that it was likely that up to a hundred families would also benefit from the munificence. It's a good job the food hygiene regulations we love today were not in existence, or the spare food would have been binned!

The charity still functions today, and its residents (twenty-five these days, not thirteen) might be easily identified because of the uniform they wear for formal occasions and attendance at the morning service in the chapel: black gowns, mediaeval hats and silver crosses. However, around the town they are usually in 'civvies', so perhaps they are not that easily spotted!

George – ever the rebel – without his hat, sunning himself on a summer's day...

Similar garb, in a mulberry colour, is worn by the second group of residents, The Order of Noble Poverty, founded three hundred years later. The words 'noble poverty' tell us that these residents were members of the nobility who had fallen on hard times.

...while John models the gown and hat for The Order of Nobel Poverty

The Hospital of St Cross, founded sometime in the middle of the 1130s, claims to be the oldest charitable institution in the United Kingdom in continuous use. Even King Henry VIII kept his fingers off!

There's another almshouse in Winchester, called St John's. Of course, there is rivalry between the two establishments, but it's not a matter of pistols at dawn – it is a set-to about which institution is the oldest. St John's claim to have an earlier foundation date is true, but it has been re-founded at a later date, as well as being merged with other charitable groups.

So, with the ball volleyed back over the net, this is speedily returned by the St Cross order, who can also boast to be the largest mediaeval almshouse in Britain. Game, set and match?

The benefactor of St Cross at its foundation was the Bishop of Winchester, that same Henry of Blois who has a posh tomb in the Cathedral, and was brother of King Stephen.

The story was that one day, when he was strolling by the river, Bishop Henry was confronted by a poor woman, carrying a baby, who – upon recognising him – fell upon her knees and begged him to help those in her neighbourhood who were suffering great hardship.

Now, apart from the king, the Bishop was the richest chap in England, so I doubt if it made much of a dent in his finances. But his charity would have helped to increase his bid for power. At the time of the foundation of St Cross, his brother Stephen was snatching the title of king, but ambitious Henry failed to get the job of Archbishop of Canterbury.

However, he outmanoeuvred everyone by getting the Pope to make him Papal Legate – a post more important than the Archbishop! So, the founding of St Cross as part of his strategy to increase his reputation and his power-base in Winchester was no bad thing.

The Church of St Cross from the Master's Garden

Trying to put an accurate date on the foundation is probably rather difficult, as do we take it from the day that he had the big idea? The day the building work began? The day people moved in? So, let's say it was about 1136!

The original building no longer stands but others, of almost the same period, are still there. It probably took a while to complete these buildings, as they were quite sturdy, and these stone homes at St Cross are still going strong and are well maintained – our present-day residents are very comfortably accommodated.

The residents have always been 'overseen' by a Master, some good and some definitely bad. One of the worst was Francis North, sixth Earl of Guilford, who misappropriated the Hospital's funds to a scandalous degree, pocketing millions (in today's value). Earl he may have been, but it just goes to show that some of those ennobled by their peers – even these days – can cream off wealth intended for those of more modest means. By going abroad with his ill-gotten gains, Francis North had no compunction to repay his 'off-shore' riches.

Passers-by are also well cared for: there is the ancient custom of the Wayfarers' Dole – pilgrims on a journey can ask for this at the Porter's Lodge and will be given a beaker of ale and some bread. So, as you start your pilgrimage towards Eastbourne, this is worth knowing.

There is also a cafeteria on-site should you wish for something a little more substantial, although it must be unique in that it apparently closes at lunchtime so that staff can have a break.

Time, I think, to be on our way!

Gargoyles keeping an eye on everyone from the beautiful transept ceiling

Oh Jerry, don't let's ask for the moon. We have the stars.

(Now, Voyager)

Near to the junction of the A31 and the A272, just to the east of the city, is Winchester Science Centre: the museum of technology, including a planetarium with the largest seating capacity in the country.

Shortly after you start your walk, you will see a large, stark, white tent-like building, rather like a pyramid. But if you are just venturing out on your personal long march, it is unlikely that you will want to be waylaid by yet another place to visit.

That's why I am mentioning it now, before I start the route.

© Courtesy of Winchester Science Centre - A hair-raising experience

It describes itself as a 'day out' 'hands-on' place, so a quick scoot around seems a little optimistic. So, with time to spare either before you start your walk, or upon its completion, here is somewhere for those of you whose thoughts are more scientific and less historical – those who enjoy seeing the stars – to indulge themselves for a few hours.

Not only does it have a massive planetarium, where you can see the heavens at any time of the day, you can see live, pioneering shows with enthusiastic presenters. Because the location has Dedicated Dark Sky status, there are amateur star-gazing events so you can see it all in real-time and for real!

© Courtesy of Winchester Science Centre - Spaced out in the centre's Planetarium

The centre has displays, many of them hands-on (so that's wonderful for children and those of us who have yet to grow up) for more than just astronomy. The biological and physical sciences get their share of the action too.

In case you are at the end of your walk and you missed out on butterflies around you as you passed by, you can remedy the loss at their on-site butterfly reserve. Among their more unusual activities, there are adult only – children banned – singles' nights. Maybe this is my chance to find 'tall, dark, handsome, can-explain-my-computer-to-me Mr Right!

So, you will find the Winchester Science Centre and Planetarium at Telegraph Way, Morn Hill, Winchester. Visible from the South Downs Way, it is a messy place to find by road, but probably worth the effort!

It's not just the scientists who love the stars, artists do too! Here's some interesting takes on the great masters, Van Gogh, Tintoretto and Titian.

Are We Nearly There Yet?

If we are going to walk the South Downs Way, perhaps it is time to get started.

This guide is not intended to direct you along the route, but to expand upon what is around you as you progress.

However, I nearly failed as soon as I had started, so to help you get on your way I will point you in the right direction. It's even confusing about where you should start. The Cathedral has, for many years, been the starting point, but now the City Mill – owned by the National Trust – seems to have taken over that role.

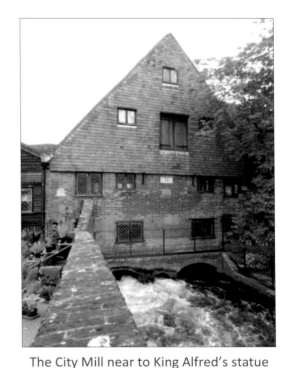

The City Mill near to King Alfred's statue

From the Cathedral, you should head East, towards the Statue of King Alfred. Happily, when you get there, the City Mill is on your left, so you can be sure that you have covered both possibilities. At that point, you will see a sign for the South Downs Way pointing along by the river – a delightful stroll. However, things went awry for me at this point.

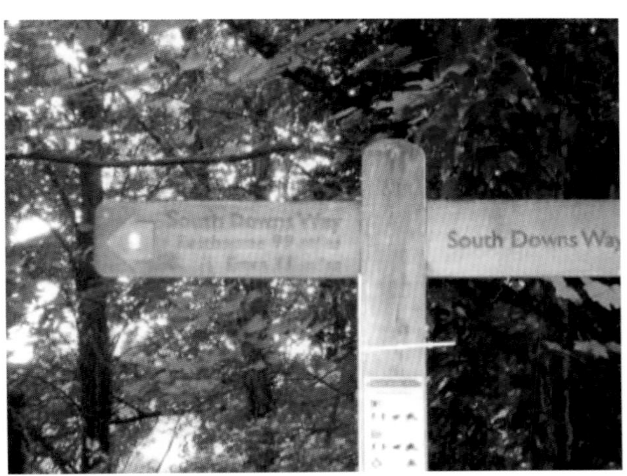

You're on your way!

If only I'd followed the footpath signs to Highcliffe when I failed to find signs for the South Downs Way, I'd have saved a great deal of time and confusion. The Highcliffe signs and St Giles Hill Viewpoint will lead you to East Hill and you will be on your way!

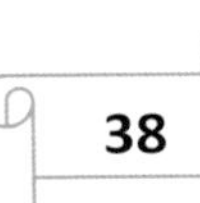

St Giles viewpoint is not far off your route, and if you wish to look back at the city of Winchester, it is a good place for this, with the bonus of an information board, indicating which buildings you can see.

It will be a great relief to find Petersfield Road, as that will lead you out of the city.

And there's more...

I've only covered some of the highlights to justify a visit. The Tourist Information Centre has maps for the area and will suggest places connected with its political, religious, or military past with a host of other places that may pique your interest.

View towards Chilcomb, taken by a passing lorry driver from his juggernaut!

Chilcomb

Ancient and Modern

Before long you will come to the small village of Chilcomb, and a signpost directs to you St Andrew's, the church. Don't worry if you hear shooting: the Ministry of Defence has a firing range just to the South of the village. You may think that World War Three is underway, but it's just practice for both the army and navy.

St Andrew's with a view of Winchester in the distance

Building of the church began shortly before the Conquest of 1066, so technically it is a Saxon church, but St Andrew's is an example of Early Norman architecture. Its simplicity and its location both make it worth a detour.

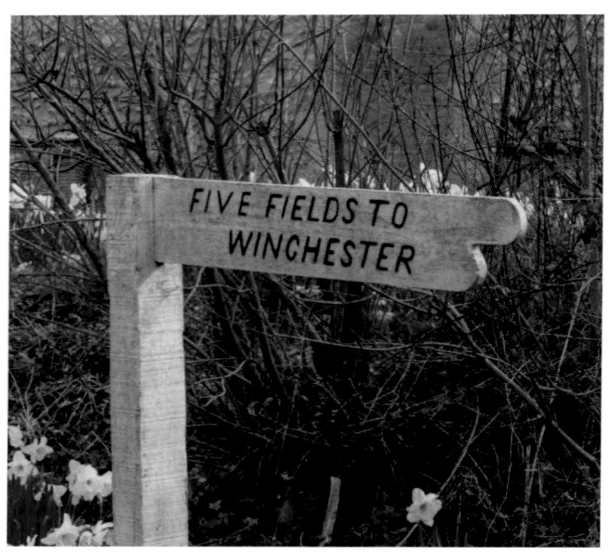

So near to the city and yet it is so tranquil!

A gateway to the car-park at the lower end of the site is clearly marked, although the church is not easily seen from the roadway.

On the day that I visited, I gave a lift to a fellow traveller, Freya, so the two of us explored the church together. With all the places that she visited on her way to Winchester with me, she certainly worked her passage!

As we made our way up the grassy path towards the church, we were struck by the poignant sight of several recent headstones for infants, babies and still-births. As visitors, we were moved by this, and it may be that you too will feel the need for a few minutes of reflection and contemplation before continuing along the path towards the church.

Considering how small Chilcomb is, it appears disproportionate how many personal tragedies are reflected by the graves. There is, however, an explanation that can, to some degree, account for the numbers. The church in Chilcomb was at one time the parish church for Highcliffe, on the outskirts of Winchester, through which the South Downs Way passed as you left the city. This is an explanation for some of the tragedies, because the parishioners who choose to use the graveyard extend beyond the village. Nevertheless, the losses felt by these families are personal griefs which are to be mourned.

As we came back down the path a while later, I recalled Ben Jonson's poem of four hundred years' ago – "On My First Sonne" – a poem reflecting the quiet dignity of the bereaved when grief cannot be hidden.

The church interior

The church itself is charming. The extreme height of the building is typical of the period. From similar buildings, it can be ascertained that the two windows, at roof level, probably contained a sanctus bell (rung as part of the Catholic Mass), as well as a larger one.

On the floor of the chancel there is a grid of nine panels containing mediaeval tiles. At the time they were known as inlaid tiles, but they were renamed encaustic tiles by the Victorians, should you wish to look up more details.

The encaustic paving

The blank tile-face would have had a deep impression of the desired pattern pushed into the surface. This was then filled with a different coloured slip (a runny mixture of the clay and water) Once it had had time to firm up a little but was still damp, cutting or scraping horizontally would reveal the completed tile that was ready to be fired in a kiln.

Currently, the church has two bells, one from 1380 when Richard II was King of England. Contrasting with this antiquity, is a modern crucifix – hanging above the Chancel arch – made from driftwood, inlayed with bronze and gilded.

Despite its peaceful setting, away from the hustle and bustle of Winchester, the church is well cared for by its Friends organisation and it still used regularly for services.

As you resume your walk, towards the East end of the village you will pass a tile-roofed granary in a private garden. This is raised above ground level in a style that has been used for centuries: staddle stones. Their mushroom-shape is difficult for rats to scale, preventing the harvest from being destroyed.

Staddle stones supporting the grain store

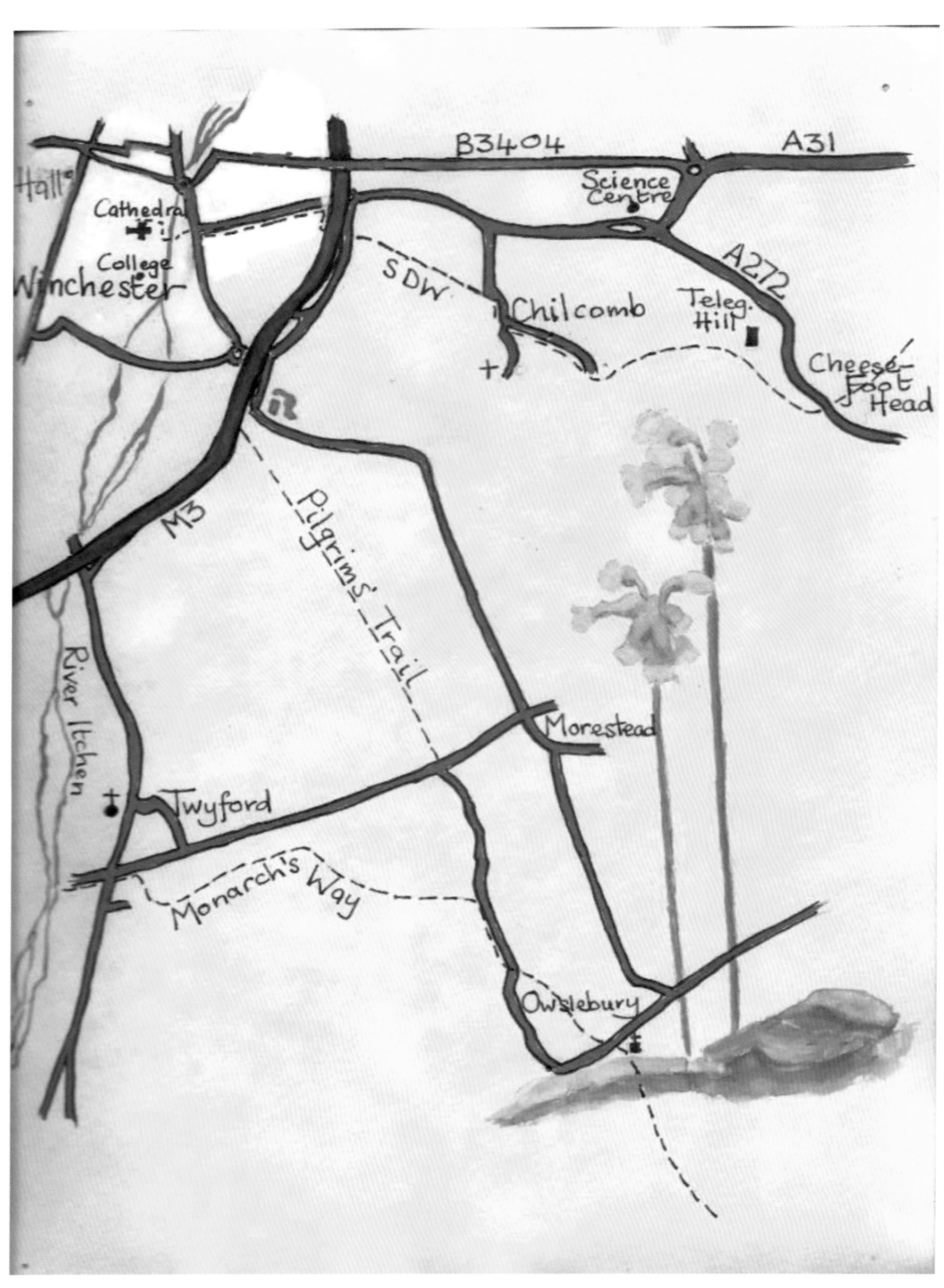
B3404
A31
Hall
Science Centre
Cathedral
College
Winchester
SDW
A272
Chilcomb
Teleg. Hill
Cheese-foot Head
M3
Pilgrims' Trail
River Itchen
Morestead
Twyford
Monarch's Way
Owslebury

Twyford and Owslebury

To Err is Human (Alexander Pope)

St Mary's at Twyford

If you're particularly interested in church architecture, and you have more leisure time on your travels – as well as transport – a few miles to the south west is Twyford with its Victorian church.

St Mary's was designed by Alfred Waterhouse, who also designed the amazing Natural History Museum in London and the very grand Town Hall in Manchester. It seems odd that a man who was designing such large, prestigious buildings should also work on a rural church and various country houses in Hampshire, but as we shall see later, he was not the only Victorian architect to have a similarly wide portfolio.

Born in Liverpool, his first practice was in Manchester before he came South to London. Perhaps, with the innovations in transport afforded by the industrial revolution, it was an opportunity not available to earlier architects. The railways provided the mobility to allow people like Waterhouse to work in Hampshire on St Mary's Church in Twyford as well as on many other buildings throughout the county.

The late twentieth century West Window

Twyford is also the village where Alexander Pope was expelled from school for writing rude things about the schoolmaster. Any teacher these days probably wishes that all such problems with pupils could be so easily remedied!

The traffic on the M3 these days shows how much the road expansion was needed

The names of Twyford and Twyford Down may be also firing off sparks in those little grey cells, recalling its frequent mention in the news in the early 1990s! The Government's plan for the M3 was left unfinished for many years because the destruction of various precious wildlife habitations in the area was considered unacceptable. The Government and the activists were in conflict for several years, and the violence from those employed to disperse the campaigners in the end enhanced the cause of the environmentalists, and it backfired on the authorities. Despite all of their efforts, the protesters did not succeed, but they did raise the profile of environmental protection in the national consciousness. So, a victory of a sort!

An Alfred Waterhouse window

Also, Brambridge House in the village was the birthplace of Maria Ann Fitzherbert, who married the Prince Regent in 1785, a marriage that was declared illegal as he was the heir to the throne and not free to choose for himself.

A little beyond Twyford is the village of Owslebury – pronounced Oz-el-berry – which although quite small can lay some claim to our attention.

Who will rid me of this turbulent priest?

Owslebury's St Andrew's Church

St Andrew's Church in Owslebury is just one of many churches along the way with 'a past'. At a time of religious turmoil in the early 1550s, the priest chose to say the Mass in Latin, which had been forbidden under the rule of King Edward VI.

The lord of the manor, Henry Seymour (brother-in-law of the former king, Henry VIII), marched into the church while the service was in progress and shot the poor vicar dead at the altar.

And as for bearing a grudge! The poor guy not only died, but his name has been omitted from the list of vicars, and to this day no one knows who he was.

The only evidence remaining is that the musket ball hit the East wall and the evidence is there for you to see!

Often there is more to discover when exploring a church, for example this beautiful memorial carving of Noah's ark and a dazzling icon of the Virgin and Child at Twyford

A-Haunting we will go...

King Henry the Eighth with wives two and three!

The Seymour connection with the village means that, if you are inclined to pay a visit to a ghost, then Jane Seymour – the only one of King Henry VIII's wives to bear him a son – is the obvious candidate. She is supposed to wander around the local manor house of Marwell Hall.

Strangely, I have also read, the vengeful spirit of Anne Boleyn is also supposed to prowl around the place, although she has no connection with the area. I can't imagine those two ladies have a very pleasant time together for eternity!

A warning to all brides!

The casket in the legend

Owslebury can also lay a claim to the Mistletoe Bride – along with several other locations in the country (another one is also in Hampshire) and at least one more in Italy. This village, however, has the evidence in the wooden chest concerned in the tragedy, which can be seen in the church.

Astonishingly, other caskets are available to be viewed elsewhere. So, as there have obviously been a great number of similar calamities, perhaps all potential brides should take note so that they can avoid such risks!

The story of Mistletoe Bride is so well-known, in Victorian times it was turned into a song that was popularly sung for many years.

Following the nuptials, a celebration was held at the home of the groom (in this case Marwell Hall). As the evening wore on, someone suggested a game of hide-and-seek. Clutching a sprig of mistletoe, the blushing bride eagerly ran off to hide... and, despite the guests searching up and down, was never seen again!

Years later, in a disused part of the house, an old chest with a self-locking lid was opened. Inside was a mildewing corpse, still holding some mistletoe!

... At length an oak chest, that had long lain hid,
Was found in the castle — they raised the lid,
And a skeleton form lay mouldering there
In the bridal wreath of that lady fair!

"The Mistletoe Bough,"
by Thomas Haynes Bayly
and Sir Henry Bishop, circa 1830

Now, these days the police would be summoned to such a mysterious disappearance and I'm there would be questions about how thorough the search had been. Upon the discovery of the corpse, I think that they would be checking for other injuries! I wonder how much the new husband inherited from the lady.

As I say, with so many mistletoe brides up and down the country, I would advise that similar games be avoided at wedding celebrations.

A peaceful scene of the nearby River Itchen

The March of Progress

However, let's get back to the village and the church. Near to the infamous wooden chest is one of two windows that were crafted in London, depicting a mother and daughter. A young Vincent van Gogh is supposed to have been inspired to take up art upon seeing these being created.

One of the pair of windows that inspired Vincent Van Gogh

The nineteenth century was a time of change: machinery was taking over from age-old methods of production: it was faster and required fewer workers, resulting in more of the product and greater profits. The other side of the coin was greater unemployment, reduced wages and greater poverty.

Villagers from Owslebury participated in the Swing Riots in 1830: a nationwide protest by agricultural workers against industrialisation of farm-work. The industrial revolution, which had destroyed the cottage industries of so many skilled crafts men and women, was encroaching upon the countryside itself, resulting in unimaginable hardship.

Mobs of agricultural workers ranged the countryside threatening to destroy machinery. These local rioters were tried in Winchester and several of them were hanged.

As a little aside, the word sabotage exists thanks to a shoe. I do like things to do with shoes! In France, the wooden clog worn by the working people is called a sabot. When the French people wrecked their machinery, they would jam the mechanism by throwing in a shoe – a sabot. Voila! The word 'sabotage' was born.

Dozy Do'h!

So far, so good! The route out of Winchester passes quite tidily through Chilcomb. However, already I can see a problem – I've now mentioned Twyford and Owslebury which are off the path and a little back on yourself. So, perhaps this is a little bit like the pantomime: "Behind you!" But...that still does not help to avoid confusion. So, I'm afraid that this task will need to be rather more like a country dance: "Swing to the right, dozy-doe your partner and swing to your left." Inevitably, I think that this could get rather messy, so as far as possible I'll try to be logical...so...let's strip the willow...

I don't believe it! This is the bridge where grumpy old Victor Meldrew was killed in the final episode of 'One Foot in the Grave'!

Telegraph Hill and Cheesefoot Head

The South Downs Way curves around, and then heads off in a South-Easterly direction, towards Cheesefoot Head. The land on the left rises gently, and upon it is a large, fairly ordinary clump of trees.

The Ordnance Survey map shows it as a rectangular blob of green. So, it is very easy to stroll straight past this apparently insignificant copse.

However, it is one of many similar sites which almost did have a real significance for the Royal Navy. Along with Cheesefoot Head, its appearance belies its true importance for military historians.

Telegraph Hill from across the A272 with a very rarely seen blue sky!

This rectangle is Telegraph Hill. In fact, in the South and East of England there are quite a few similarly named high spots which were all part of a plan by The Admiralty to develop a communications system between the headquarters in London and its maritime ports. Not accessible by footpath, the land is not the highest point in the area, as you might expect. However, in previous centuries – without the trees – it would have provided clear views to the West, beyond

Winchester, and also towards the North East, itself being clearly visible from those directions. Apart from its name, however, there is nothing to indicate its significance.

Although the Admiralty's initial scheme had been abandoned before our Telegraph Hill could be used as intended, it was still used for a short while as part of a revised development in communications.

In the first instance, the scheme that the Royal Navy had wanted to put into effect had been, ironically, a French innovation (the concept of Monsieur Claude Chappe). The use of the Admiralty Shutter System aimed to reduce the time taken to send messages between the Admiralty in London to the Royal Navy ports in Deal, Yarmouth, Portsmouth and Plymouth. With the war against the French, good communications were important.

The Portsmouth system was a resounding success, reducing the time for a message to get through from a number of hours to approximately the same number of minutes.

The location of the signalling station from Winchester Science Centre

At least – as we shall see later – it worked magnificently in unfoggy weather and not at night. There was also difficulty in windy conditions. And in freezing weather the shutters would stick. So, with good ol' English weather, there were no problems then!

Similar in concept to the binary system (the on/off coding system used in computer technology), an array of six shutters, allowing sixty-three permutations - would display letters of the alphabet, numbers and key words. A line of signalling stations, on high hills, repeated the message along a course through the countryside towards its destination.

Yes – the on/off system used for computers these days was used over two hundred years ago. It was used even earlier for the jacquard looms in France, producing elaborate silk fabrics for the heavy brocade dresses of fashionable ladies (the sort of ladies who were probably thrilled with their beautiful gowns and shortly afterwards lost their heads in excitement!). The binary coding system was also used for music boxes and pianolas! Il n'y a rien de nouveau sous le soleil!

The Portsmouth line was already proving its worth when Napoleon was captured and imprisoned on Elba. With the urgency gone, the plan for the route to Plymouth was abandoned and the Portsmouth link was closed down for a few days, although it was then reopened with a simpler system.

Just as everyone was resigning themselves to peace, Napoleon had the gall to escape, landing in France at the beginning of May, 1815. However, just over six weeks later the Duke of Wellington's troops defeated Napoleon at Waterloo. He was imprisoned and later died on St Helena on 5th May, 1821.

By the time the branch-line to Plymouth was partially put into operation (it never did get all the way), the cumbersome screens, looking perhaps rather like cricket sight-screens on hill tops, had been abandoned in favour of semaphore signalling, requiring a man (or a 'mechanical' man) with a couple of flags. Coming from North Kent, I was interested to learn that the first use by the Royal Navy of semaphore communications was between Chatham and Sheerness.

Hampshire Chronicle

Monday, April 6th, 1829

Winchester. — The Commissioners of the Navy are about to erect a new line of semaphores, in order to accelerate the communication with Plymouth. The eminence called Chestford Head, near this city, has been selected as one of the stations, on which a residence will shortly be built for the accommodation of the officer and men to be stationed there.

Hampshire Chronicle

Monday, May 17th, 1830

Winchester.—The semaphore building on Cheesefoot Head, near this city, is now completed. Three others, in the same line of communication, are about to be erected at Farley, Sherfield English and Woodfield Green.

Although the semaphore method of communication did not instantly fade into obscurity (I remember learning it in the Girl Guides – fortunately, with my spelling, I was never required to use it: I dread to think what sort of message would have been received!), it was still limited to clear daytime usage.

So, although our Telegraph Hill had a short 'productive life', once the railways came into being, it was far easier to send messages by rail. Not as quick as signalling, the railways could be used whatever the time or the weather (almost: heaven forbid that there should be leaves on the line), and the messages could be more detailed.

Before long, even this method of communication was abandoned in favour of Morse Code. Now? Well… anytime, anyplace, anywhere with "me mobile"!

Now, Telegraph Hill is just a clump of trees.

What a Brie(s)! Cheesefoot Head

Trying to remember which way round the body parts go in the name Cheesefoot Head is a real pain in the neck! The 'cheese' part does not refer to a nice bit of Cheddar or Wensleydale, but is a corruption of the word 'chesil' as in Chesil Beach, further to the West. In both instances it is derived from the Old English ceosel or cisel, which means gravel or shingle and is, therefore, a description of the local geology. The 'foot' part couldn't be more obvious: it is simply the foot or bottom of a hill! Just to make things awkward again, it is pronounced 'Chezzit' Head.

As the footpath traverses the Eastern edge, the large grassy bowl beside you is impressive, although it is only from the opposite direction that the way the landscape cuts away can be truly appreciated.

This natural area has formed a dramatic background on many occasions.

What a load of rubbish!

Over the centuries, Cheesefoot Head has been used in various ways, recently as a venue for music concerts. For example, since 2009, the Boomtown Festival has been held here each summer. Audiences of sixty thousand can be accommodated in this amphitheatre.

The organisers donate some of the profits to charity and the majority of the people have a fantastic time. However, a proportion of the crowd tarnish what should be an excellent occasion for all.

Take drugs. No, that's not a suggestion, it's a problem! When the police confiscate £80,000 worth of drugs and a further £55,000 is handed in, it raises the question how much was not handed over? What with eighty cars destroyed by fire, there are people whose memories of the occasion will not be so good.

Almost two weeks after the festival, the clearing up goes on

Of course, the disruption to the lives of those who live and work on the surrounding area is also to be considered. So many visitors focusing on such a restricted area cannot but cause traffic problems, and I suppose it is not surprising that over a week later the arena

was still scarred by the detritus of the occasion. Sadly, those few whose motives are not, well, let's just say 'above board' can make the lives of the neighbours particularly miserable.

Nevertheless, such a wonderful location is appreciated by the majority of those at Boomtown, and other functions have also brought great pleasure to thousands of people, including the locals.

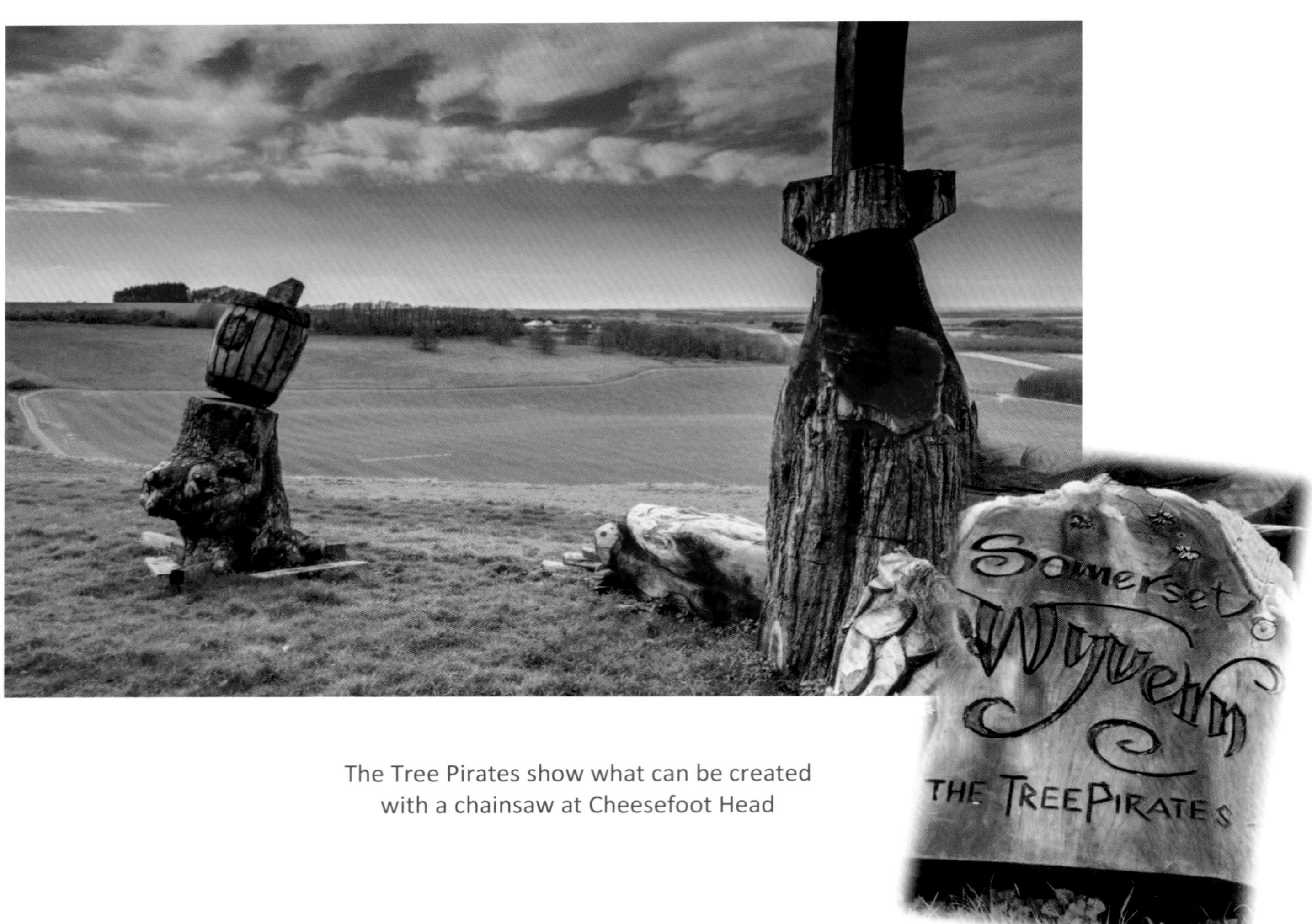

The Tree Pirates show what can be created with a chainsaw at Cheesefoot Head

Friends, Romans, countrymen: lend me your (cauliflower) ears!

(from Julius Caesar - almost – Wm. Shakespeare)

Towards the South Downs Way, illustrating the natural bowl in the landscape

During the Second World War, the boxer Joe Louis travelled from America to visit the GIs stationed in the area. He entertained them with a boxing match, the sloping sides of the arena giving a good view of the event for the audience.

As the war progressed, the United States officially joined the Allied forces in December 1941. In the months leading up to the D-Day Landings in 1944, thousands of American

troops were encamped throughout Hampshire, waiting for the big day. The leafy woodlands provided ideal camouflage, masking the huge number of soldiers from being spotted by any enemy reconnaissance flights. Equipment was similarly disguised.

Don't tell 'em, Pike!

from Dad's Army: David Croft and Jimmy Perry

Strangely, the complete opposite was happening over in Kent. The Whitehall Boffins devised plans to convince the Nazis that the big push would be from Kent towards Calais. Subterfuge was needed: 'information' was leaked to spies and informants to reinforce the evidence that could be seen on the ground. For example, equipment – including tanks – was clearly visible on the chalk downs near Dover.

Inflatable tank (Crown copyright)

The catch was these were either timber or inflatable decoy tanks. It just seems the sort of scheme that Captain Mainwaring and his boys would have concocted. But it worked!

Back in Hampshire, the waiting and preparation went on – the armed forces from Britain, America and the British Empire, including Canada and India (now known as the Commonwealth) were ready for action.

Almost overnight, the countryside of Hampshire became denuded as the combined forces set off for the beaches of Normandy on 6th June, 1944.

Once More Unto the Beach, Dear Friends...

Henry the Fifth; – almost – Wm. Shakespeare

But let's go back briefly to Cheesefoot Head just before the big push. Whereas King George VI was further East in the county saluting the British and Empire troops, General Dwight D Eisenhower came to Cheesefoot Head. It was here that he addressed the American GIs with the requisite motivational speech before they embarked for the Normandy beaches.

Once More Unto the Breech, Dear Friends...

Ibid.

Although Shakespeare tells us that King Henry V did his motivational speech at Agincourt, in fact he made his preparations for battle, and probably addressed his troops, in Hampshire in 1415 – before they crossed the Channel – at nearby Portchester Castle. Until Portsmouth became a major military port, Portchester was favoured by the English kings as their command centre.

As a child, watching Lawrence Olivier on television in the film of 'Henry the Fifth', I mistakenly thought that the King had proclaimed 'Once more unto the beach, dear friends'.

At the age of five, this sounded like the best idea ever, and I have been a fan of William Shakespeare ever since!

Portchester Castle, not far from the M27 to the North East of Portsmouth – day and evening

Tichborne

From Cheesefoot Head the route continues for just over three miles on the North side of the A272 before dropping down to the South side again.

However, while we are on that side, perhaps there is time to venture into a few other places. For example, off to the Northwest is the town of Alresford, and on your way there you'll find the village of Tichborne.

For this relatively small village – with fewer than two hundred inhabitants – Tichborne can lay claim to two stories involving two people of the same name, more than seven hundred years apart: Sir Roger Tichborne. But more of these two gents later.

As well as these two, a family member was executed at the Tower of London in 1586 for treason. He had the unusual name of Chidiock Tichborne (often called Charles) who was a conspirator in the Babington Plot: a scheme to murder Elizabeth I and instate Mary Queen of Scots onto the throne.

There is also a tragic drowning to add to the family's woes.

Where to start? At the very beginning...alphabetically...a very good place to start!

Eyes, look your last!

A Midsummer Night's Dream: Wm. Shakespeare

Chidiock Tichborne is better known for the poem he wrote in the hours before his death than for being a major player in the political intrigues of the late Tudor era. Condemned to death for plotting against Queen Elizabeth I, he was imprisoned in the Tower of London to await his fate. On the 19th September 1586 this young man wrote 'Tichborne's Elegy, an eighteen line poem, rather introspectively mourning his early death when he had so much more to live for. Mind you, at a moment so close to their demise, I doubt many people would be writing comic verse!

Had he done so, perhaps it would have gone something like this:

There was a young man called Chidiock
Who felt like a bit of an idiot!
Parting his head from neck
Would leave him a wreck,
And all for the sake of a silly plot!

Poorly rhyming, poorly scanning, I doubt if this would have been remembered in the annals of great poetry.

The real poem goes like this:

My Elegy by Chidiock

My prime of youth is but a frost of cares,
My feast of joy is but a dish of paine,
My Crop of corne is but a field of tares,
And al my good is but vaine hope of gaine.
The day is past, and yet I saw no sunne,
And now I live, and all my life is done.

My tale was heard, and yet it was not told,
My fruite is falne, & yet my leaves are greene:
My youth is spent, and yet I am not old,
I saw the world, and yet I was not seene.
My thred is cut, and yet it is not spunne,
And now I live, and now my life is done.

I sought my death, and found it in my wombe,
I lookt for life, and saw it was in shade:
I trod the earth and knew it was my Tombe,
And now I die, and now I was but made.
My glasse is full, and now my glasse is runne,
And now I live, and now my life is done.

Executions were not a neat job with a sharp axe. It generally involved being hanged, drawn and quartered which involved removing the half dead victim from the gallows, leaving him to observe (and feel), the drawing bit (having his guts removed). Finally, came the quartering bit: the mutilation of his body.

It must have been a relief to have fainted and so have been unaware of your final moments. However, those waiting in line for their turn would have seen it all.

When Queen Elizabeth I heard of the first day's horror, she was so gutted she insisted that the victims should remain on the gibbet until they were dead. I'm sure that they were grateful for the reprieve!

A Momentary Diversion... before returning to the local gentry

Elevated upon a hill in the village is the church of St Andrew's, a simple building from the eleventh century, with later additions. It's in a beautiful location, with wonderful views over the neighbouring countryside.

Inside, the nave has Jacobean box pews, one with the coat of arms of the Tichborne family. As a feature, I find the pews rather forbidding, as the style separates the congregation into groups and gives the building a rather enclosed feeling. Of course, in times gone by, the wealthier families would have felt their privileged position in society could be better enjoyed by keeping the lower classes further away from them.

God made them high and lowly, and ordered their estate.

However, in the days when the vicar might well give a sermon lasting for an hour or more, the advantage of box-pews for the younger children throughout the congregation was the chance to play with a doll or some lead soldiers! These days I am sure many celebrants would find it useful for various telecommunications devices, while the youngsters have electronic games that they can play.

Unsurprisingly, the church at Tichborne – St Andrew's – has memorials to the Tichborne family. Rather more remarkable is a Roman Catholic chapel inside this Protestant church. Since the time of Henry VIII, the established faith in this country – at first English Catholicism – has been firmly Protestant (with a couple of hiccups in the reigns of Mary I – 1554 to 1558 – and James II – 1685 to 1688).

The monarchy has maintained the faith, and laws dictate the status quo should remain. The secular state remained staunchly protestant until quite recently when acts of Parliament were required before those of other faiths could take up positions in government and our larger institutions. When Catholic priests and the practice of the Latin Mass or other holy rituals could lead to imprisonment of death, it seems an anomaly that a Roman Catholic chapel should sit so comfortably alongside the Established Church of England.

Memorial for Sir Benjamin Tichborne and his wife Amphillis in the Catholic Chapel at Tichborne Church

A tomb must cover thy sweet eyes

A Midsummer Night's Dream: Wm. Shakespeare

But let's return to the turbulent lives of the Tichborne family. Within St Andrew's Church is a memorial – dated 1619 – to a very junior member of the clan: Richard, who died aged "one yeare six monethes and too daies". The monument has the boy asleep, robed in red, his head resting upon a puffed-up pillow.

Not for the first time in this family's history the infant's death involved some cursing! The legend tells of a gypsy woman who begged for food at the house but was turned away. Angered, she swore that baby Richard should die by drowning on a particular day. For the child's safety, the family insured that he should not go near to water on that day.

Nevertheless, an outing in his perambulator turned to disaster as the wheel caught in a rut on the lane and the carriage toppled over, casting the child into a small puddle where the curse was fulfilled.

I can't believe that it took more than a few seconds to pick up the child, which does make the whole tale seem pretty remarkable.

Young Richard's memorial

What dreadful Dole is here?

A Midsummer Night's Dream: Wm. Shakespeare

King Stephen's reign was dogged by civil war, as his cousin Matilda seemed to have a stronger claim to the throne, as the only legitimate direct heir of King Henry I. A determined woman, she had fought hard to claim her birthright, but as a female, she had a battle against a patriarchal society. Nevertheless, it was a turbulant nineteen years (1135 -1154) until an agreement was reached between the two factions that it would be Matilda's son, Henry, who would acceed to the throne.

During this time, another strong-willed woman lived in Tichborne. She was tenacious in her final battle against her malicious husband and also in combatting her physical frailty. Perhaps it was a reflection of the cruelty of the times, or perhaps he was a harbinger of the typical Victorian melodramatic villain: who knows? What is important to the villagers of Tichborne, is that she took him on and won!

Lady Mabel was the wife of the first of our infamous Sir Roger Tichbornes. During this time of unrest, when wars and battles would have destroyed families and farms, Lady Mabel Tichborne took to her bed, a wasting disease confining her there for many years. By 1150, she knew her time was short.

The Tichborne Dole (1671) by Gillis van Tilborch

She was obviously moved by the plight of the poor. With Winchester so close, the political unrest must have ravaged the homes and livelihoods of those nearby. So, her dying bequest to her husband was to make an annual 'dole' (donation) of food to those in need by setting aside some land to finance this.

Her parsimonious husband refused.

As a spark of generosity, he conceded that any land his morbidly sick wife could crawl around in the time it took a log to burn in the fire grate would be assigned to her cause.

So, Mabel had herself carried to the most fertile land on the estate and the log was ignited. She then crawled around an area of twenty three acres (I understand that you could fit thirteen standard football pitches inside a space that big) before the log was consumed!

Even then, she could not trust her devoted spouse to fulfil her bequest. So, as you do, she made a curse!

Should the annual distribution of the dole on Lady Day (25th March) be discontinued, the Lord of the Manor would sire seven sons, but the next generation would be seven daughters (and as we know from Queen Matilda's fate, that was not good news inheritance-wise). The icing on the cake would be the destruction of the house and the demise of the family name.

How's that for top trumps?

So, how did things turn out? Well, Sir Roger and his heirs ensured that the Tichborne Dole was maintained.

That is, until Sir Henry abolished it in 1799...and in 1803 part of the house fell down and the remainder was demolished!

As if this was not warning enough, the next incumbent of the title in 1821 (one of seven sons) had seven daughters. Thus it was the Dole was reinstated and continues to this day.

There was a possible blip in 1947 when the rationing rules continuing from World War Two resulted in a shortage of coupons for 'bread units'. The Government nearly came to the rescue, but publicity again roused the 'Dunkirk Spirit' among the people of Britain and bread units were donated by people throughout the country to enable the annual distribution to continue. Although this was illegal, the Government turned a blind eye.

So despite the dastardly Sir Roger, this is definitely a tale with a happy ending!

The law, the law upon his head!

A Midsummer Night's Dream: Wm. Shakespeare
...otherwise known as The Tichborne Trials

It's ironic that, only one year after Charles Dickens completed his novel 'Bleak House', real life events in Hampshire were just beginning which would echo a central theme of the book – a legal case that dragged on for decades. In the book the various claimants of Jarndyce versus Jardyce were dragged down through misery, mayhem and madness.

The cause célèbre that began in this small village in Hampshire, involving a family who lived quietly away from the politics and social whirl in London, became known as the Tichborne Claimant and involves our second Sir Roger. The case ended in 1874 and was, until recently, the longest case in British legal history, at 188 days.

This Roger Tichborne was born in 1829 and the only remarkable thing about him was a rarely mentioned medical condition (undescended genitalia). In those days, most boys were not put into trousers until they were aged about five, but young Roger was kept in skirts until he was aged twelve in the hope that his sweet chariot would swing low! Not really the sort of problem most men would want publicised! This, however, was a key piece of evidence in years to come.

He often spent time staying with his aunt and uncle, where he and his cousin, Katherine, fell in love. Both sides of the family objected, one reason being the close blood relationship.

Heartbroken, Roger travelled overseas. At first, he spent more than a year in South America before leaving impulsively for the West Indies in 1854. The ship – the Bella – was never seen again and Roger was presumed dead. His younger brother, Alfred, inherited the family's title and wealth.

The current Tichborne House with the family dog on guard

Nevertheless, his demise was not accepted by his mother, who advertised in this country and abroad for information. His dissolute brother then died at the age of just twenty seven, leaving a wife who was pregnant with the necessary male heir!

No wonder Charles Dickens thought that this sort of thing was an intriguing sort of story for his 1853 novel, and got in first! I wouldn't be surprised if the script writers of the television soaps haven't considered it!

Twelve years had slipped by when Roger Tichborne made contact from Australia, where he had built a new life for himself as a butcher and postman.

The biggest (!) evidence that this man had to support his claim was that he had the same genital malformation as the missing man. Most people would dismiss the man's claim as entirely speculative, but with medical evidence like that, you couldn't really dismiss it with a rude word beginning with b!

To be or not to be – the Claimant, Roger Tichborne

The delighted mother invited the resurrected Roger to England with his family.

Now, after all that introduction, we get to the case in law. Roger, having been declared dead, his nephew had inherited everything.

Thus it was that Tichborne versus Tichborne began.

Inconveniently for the Claimant, his greatest supporter – Roger's mother – died.

Not a rich man, he had to raise money for his case, so he sold speculative shares to the public, which raised the profile of the case even more. International enquiries take money and time, but there was one more piece of evidence which, in the end, caused the tide of popular support amongst the upper classes to ebb away.

Asked about the contents of a package Roger had left with a friend before his departure, he explained in open court that it contained instructions to help his youthful amour – Kitty – should she have been pregnant. To malign a lady by suggesting her youthful passion may have got the better of her, shocked the upper classes so much the trial collapsed. The Claimant was declared to be a fraud and was arrested for perjury.

It is said that all publicity is good publicity, which may be why, to raise funds, our Roger took to the stage. Music Hall appearances and ephemera for sale raised his celebrity profile. His good looks won him many female supporters.

The perjury trial, a national sensation, was overseen by no less than the Lord Chief Justice of England. Grub Street loved it! Even so, he was sentenced to fourteen years' hard labour. But, though from the public eye, support continued to grow for his case. Eventually, however, the story became old news and people's interest waned.

When he died, he was buried in a pauper's grave. However, five thousand people went to the funeral in Paddington Cemetery and even more lined the route of his funeral cortege.

Strangely, when you consider the enmity in the family, his coffin had a plate attached – with the family's acquiescence – stating "Sir Roger Charles Doughty Tichborne". Which poses the question: was he or was he not the real Roger?

Alresford

By now, you 're probably slumped over a pint at the Tichborne Arms, overwhelmed by the story of everyday country-folk. Needing the bright lights, a visit to the nearby town of Alresford might not go amiss.

There are plenty of places to eat and drink in town, although the range of shops is not extensive. If you 're into interior design or ladies' fashion, then your choice is quite wide. With a small supermarket, a chemist and a hardware shop, most people's needs can be met.

Today, Alresford is a major centre for the growing of watercress, a process requiring lots of clear water, and it is water that's behind much of the development of this town over the centuries.

Whereas Winchester put Hampshire on the map politically through its status in Mediaeval times, and its cathedral gave the area spiritual prominence, it is Alresford that can illustrate agricultural and economic life in the county from the end of the twelfth century.

A Fishy Tale

In the first few months of the reign of King Richard I (The Lionheart), Godfrey de Luci was enthroned as the Bishop of Winchester. But from what I know about Richard I, he probably was more interested in the Crusades than his kingdom, so we don't need to worry about him!

It has been speculated that Godfrey devised a plan to bring prosperity to the area by making the rivers Alre and Itchen navigable (the plan may originally have been the brain-child of Henri of Blois who we came across in Winchester, but nothing came of it then). In all likelihood, the creation of a dam was needed to regulate the water-flow.

Conveniently, this created a fish pond right by one of the Bishop's palaces! So it is quite possible the fish bit was more important than the navigation bit. With the large number of Holy Days each year when the eating of meat was prohibited, fish ponds were very desirable.

A small peek at the enormous pond in Alresford

The construction of the weir resulted in Old Alresford Pond. These days it's used for leisure as well as being a habitat for wildlife, although it is a lot smaller than it was, at only sixty acres instead of the two hundred acres it covered in Mediaeval times – that is a lot of fish!

Controlling the water-flow along the river banks meant that mills built there could be powered by water.

The Daily Grind

Of course, the grinding of wheat, highly regulated by the land owners, enabled the production of flour, which was essential to feed the population.

Would Ewe Believe It!

However, there was a second type of mill that benefitted the area, one that allowed the countryside around it to participate in one of the largest economic successes in England throughout the centuries: wool.

Arable farming kept the population fed, but was quite labour intensive. This was fine when the feudal system meant a cheap workforce would not only toil in their own fields but also on the land of the liege-lords.

As time went by, these social and legal systems changed and landowners realised that grazing was more profitable. Fewer labourers were needed to maintain flocks of sheep, providing meat and leather as well as – most profitably of all – wool. Largely driven by the monasteries, it was the creator of England's wealth and one of its greatest exports.

The wool, once sheared, needed to undergo various processes (dyeing, spinning, and weaving are just three) before it became fabric ready to be tailored. Several of the stages needed large quantities of water, including fulling in the mill in Alresford.

Once the cloth was woven, it still had a very 'thready' appearance, not the smooth undrafty fabric we might expect. So, to fluff up the fibres the woven cloth had to be beaten about a bit – it was fulled. This was done using water and large wooden hammers. This felting also helped the fabric become a little more water-resistant.

The dirty, greasy (just think how oily your hair gets if you don't wash it) fabric needed to be cleaned – scoured - before being fulled. Chemicals were used for these processes: including urine! Yes, people were paid to hand over buckets of the stuff for quite a few industrial processes. And we just flush it away! Before the process was mechanised, the fulling would be done by trampling.

That's what I call 'putting your foot in it'.

Some of the many sheep breeds that you'll find on your travels around the Hampshire countryside ... and probably at the butcher's too!

Having made a right mess of the fabric, it would then be stretched back to shape on large frames called tenters, attached by hooks and just left hanging around. So next time you are left hanging around in suspense, you'll understand why you've been left on 'tenterhooks'!

Alresford's fulling mill straddles the River Itchen

The mill in Alresford, dating from those very early years, can be found by following signs to the riverside walk. After a few twists and turns, this ancient building can be seen, straddling the river. It's not open to the public, having been rescued and restored in the middle of the twentieth century and turned into a private home.

Over the centuries, careful cross-breeding has developed sheep producing different grades of wool: shorter fibres for knitting and longer ones for weaving, which means that the fulling mill has been largely eliminated from the manufacturing process. With worsted fabric, the longer fibres mean that fulling is unnecessary.

With the Industrial Revolution, from the eighteenth century machines took over from men. A rotary machine was patented in 1833. Progress continued and now it's like magic: the fabric goes in one end of a machine, lots of processes take place as the wand is waved and ... "Izzy wizzy, let's get busy": out comes the completed cloth, just like that. Now, "That's magic!"

What's in a name?

Romeo and Juliet; Wm. Shakespeare

As towns and villages grew, it became useful to have surnames to distinguish one man from another with the same Christian name. So it was that a man's employment might have been adopted as his family name, the name that has gone down through the centuries and can give people information about their ancestors. For example, 'Fuller' would tell you the man worked in a fulling mill, like the one in Alresford. From the pre-mechanisation of this process comes the name Walker, as does Tucker, depending on which part of the country they lived in. The Welsh place-name Pandy comes from the same process.

Other surnames come from the wool trade: Shepherd, Shearer, Spinner, Weaver and Taylor are just a few.

Other crafts and skills also provided names that are familiar to us today. Mr Archer may be obvious, but he wouldn't have got far without Messrs. Fletcher, Stringer and Bowman. The building trades give us Messrs. Mason, Thatcher, Tyler and Wright among others. Mr. Cooper made the barrels and Mr Brewer filled them. The list goes on and on. When you add personal qualities (for example, Armstrong) and where people lived (Mr Oakley's home was sheltered by an oak tree) so many other names seem obvious!

A Delicate Truth

Book title by John Le Carré

There are some places that, well, one wouldn't usually mention in a book about...oh: what the...let's just say it...I'm about the mention the public toilet!

Well, most places bearing a plaque are monuments or homes, but not in Alresford. Here it's the gents' toilet that has the claim to fame, opposite the former police station, down the turning towards the railway station.

Now, most councils would poo-poo the idea of commemorating the location where spies, during the Cold War, left and received little messages. Alresford, however, is obviously flushed with pride about its connection. The Russians seem to have had a cistern – a chain of command – for the movement of information.

Now: don't be po-faced about this: you can sniff out the location if you visit the town. And before you ask: no, I did not get this story about the syphoning off of government secrets from WikiLeaks.

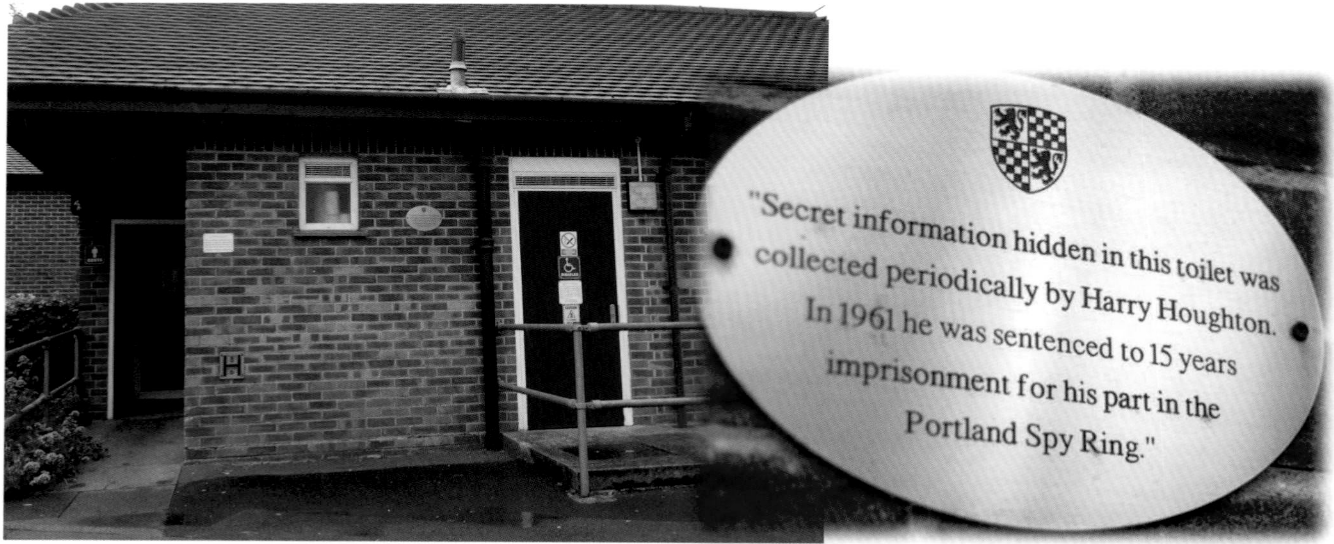

"Secret information hidden in this toilet was
collected periodically by Harry Houghton.
In 1961 he was sentenced to 15 years
imprisonment for his part in the
Portland Spy Ring."

It wasn't a deposit you'd have expected at this location: the gents' toilet with the commemorative plaque

The information comes from a book by Harry Houghton, who was a member of the Portland Spy Ring:

> *I was given instructions that at any time I received literature through the post about Renault cars, such as a brochure about new models, I was to hold it up to the light and examine it thoroughly. If there was a pin hole through the centre I was to go into the gents' lavatory at Alresford...enter (the cubicle) on the left, take out a package which I would find behind the door...and proceed to London.*

Once in the city, the place of exchange was another toilet! Could they claim that they were only following ordures?

Britain's secrets were draining away, going down the pan.

The group was arrested early in 1961 and Houghton was imprisoned until 1970. In 1964, the film Ring of Spies was produced and he was played by Bernard Lee (Mmmmm!).

Moving on...

AMBLE 353m
BOOT 308m
STILEWAY 92m
GATESIDE 501m
SOCKBURN 296m
CORNEY 312m
NETTLEBED 62m
SPLATT 178m

If you've chosen to stay on the South Downs Way rather than taken the diversion up to Alresford, you'll soon turn towards the South and be ready to re-cross the A272 and head off towards The Milburys.

However, there may be another little diversion that will pique your interest before you reach the main road. The South Downs Way takes a very sharp turn, which can be easily missed if you are chatting with companions. That lapse in concentration will lead you off past the Hockleys (you can see where you are heading with a quick look at your OS map).

The good news is that there's no need to panic – instead, you will have the chance to discover a battlefield, two haunted houses – one decidedly hostile – a beautiful garden and a church with a difference.

Dramatic skies and a sun-dappled Hampshire landscape

And, should you wish, you can re-join the A272 at a different point from the official walk, and this change of route takes you to Cheriton with a well-known battle-ground from the English Civil War and a modern-day spat over the name of an adjoining village!

A hop, skip and a jump further down the A272 is Hinton Ampner with a story to send shivers down the spine of even the most cynical of readers.

South of here is the village of Kilmeston...where the manor house has links with the Civil War in a surprising way.

Another delightful diversion can be taken if you prefer to continue a short way further along the A272, where you will come to Bramdean, with a gorgeous garden which is very rarely open to the public, and also a most unusual church from Victorian times.

For those of you eager to be on your way, however, then you can skip this bit and get back to our footpath, the South Downs Way and the change in direction to the South. You may prefer to continue on towards Beauworth, the Milbury's, Preshaw, Betty Mundy's Bottom, Lomer, Beacon Hill and Exton.

Meanwhile, the rest of us will take a break and re-join you later!

Never so weary, never so in woe...
I can no further crawl, no further go

A Midsummer Night's Dream; Wm Shakespeare

Whereas I ambled along with a day-bag on my back, others take a great deal more, including everything bar the kitchen sink. You may be one who has your tent and overnight stuff with you, making your journey rather more strenuous.

If so, not only will these diversions have to wait until another day, you may well be anxious to get to your first stop. So, keep on the South Downs Way and cross the A272,

A welcome sight for many walkers

as almost straight away you will reach Holden Farm, where tents can be pitched and a relaxing shower enjoyed.

Originally, the name of this farm was Holding (not Holden) Farm, and it did just that! Stockmen leading their animals to market in Winchester would stop at Holding Farm for the night, so that both man and beast could rest before entering the city. Greatly revived, the animals would be friskier and healthier, and likely to get a better price at the auction.

Hopefully, you will emerge from your tent feeling friskier too, and ready to continue on your way past Beauworth and to meet up with those of us who've gone via Cheriton when we come back to the South Downs Way along the Wayfarers' Walk.

Good morning, campers!

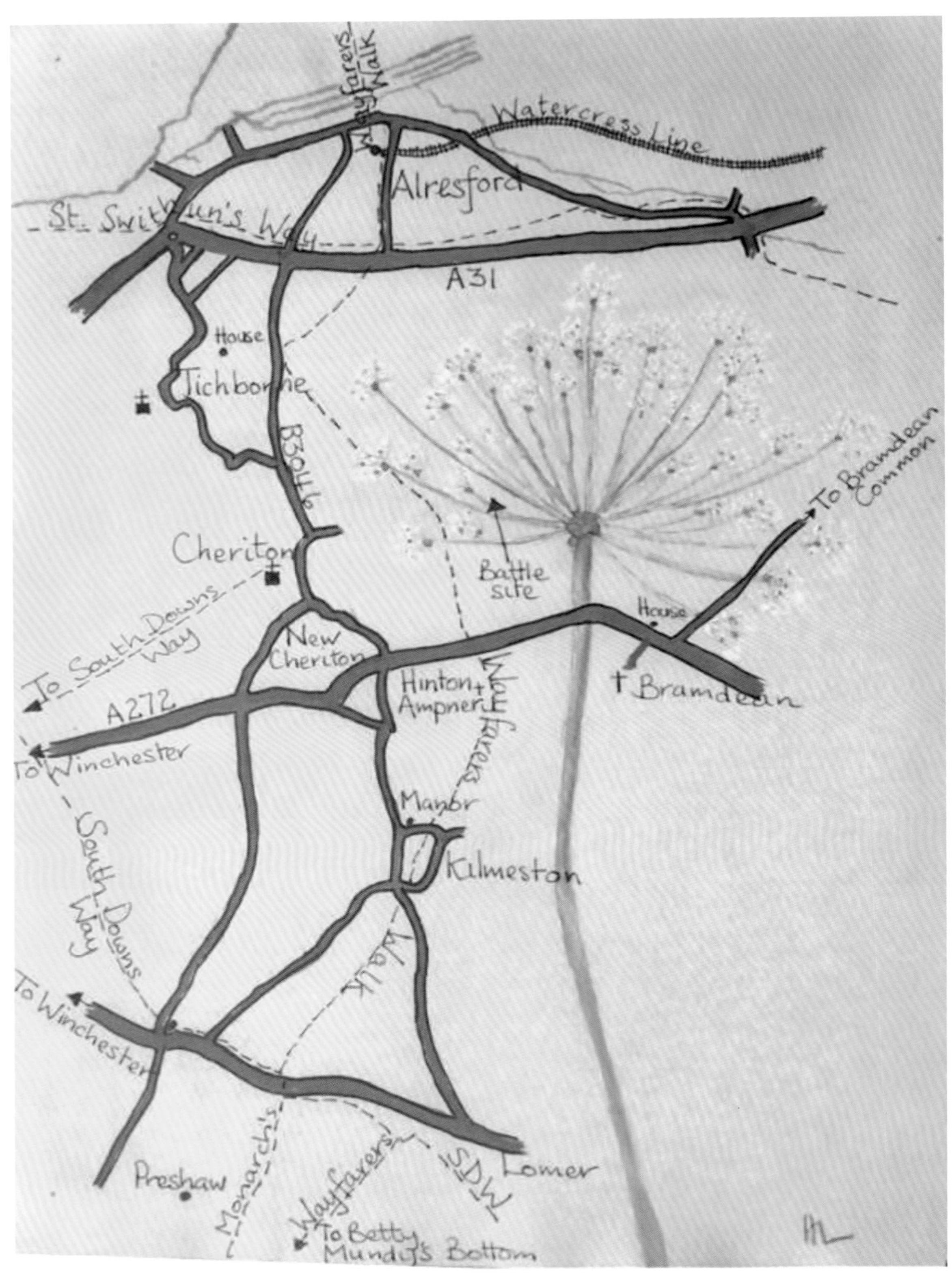
Wayfarers Walk
Watercress Line
Alresford
St. Swithun's Way
A31
House
Tichborne
B3046
Cheriton
Battle site
To Bramdean Common
House
To South Downs Way
New Cheriton
Hinton Ampner
Bramdean
A272
To Winchester
Wayfarers
Manor
Kilmeston
South Downs Way
Walk
To Winchester
Preshaw
Monarch's
Wayfarers
SDW
Lomer
To Betty Mundy's Bottom

Hinton Marsh and New Cheriton

One Place, Two Names

Confusing though this may be, this is not a sequel to the stage show "One Man, Two Guvnors". This is about a village that is so close to Cheriton that, as both have grown over the years, they now brush cheek to cheek. Nevertheless, the good folk of Hinton Marsh are quite clear they are not an outpost of their larger neighbour.

It has been mooted that the confusion has been caused by a conspiracy of jealous rivals in the Best Kept Village Competition. By suggesting that the less prettified Hinton Marsh is part of Cheriton, it might reduce their marks and break the stranglehold the larger village has on the title – three times by 2004. Surely not!

To some of us, both villages have their attractions!

Cheriton

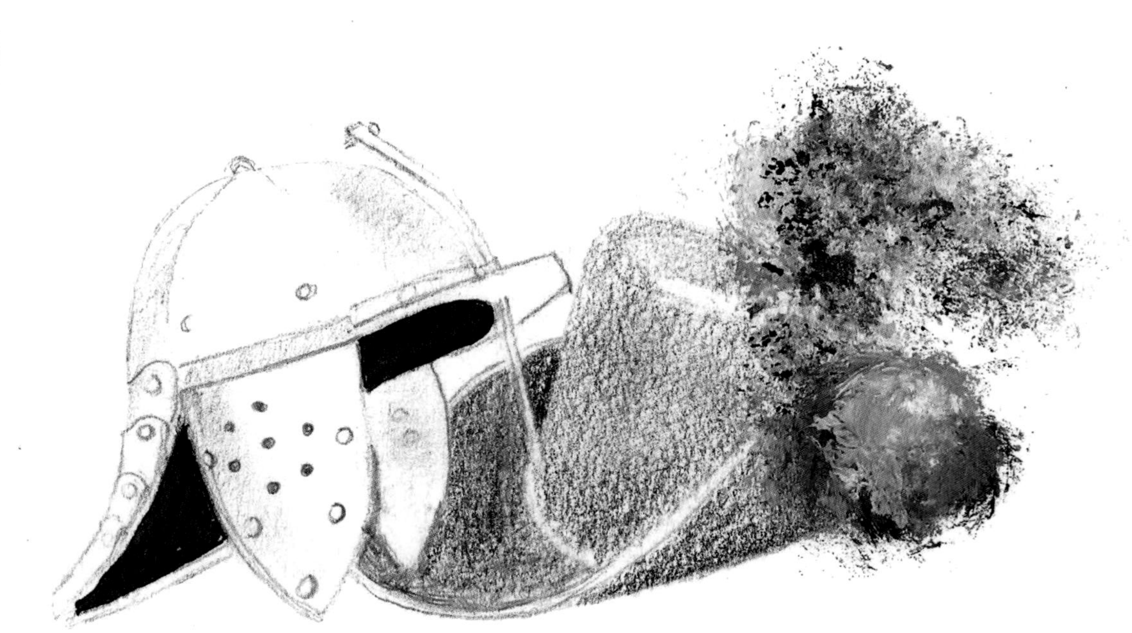

A Not-So-Very Civil War

Although we all think of this conflict as 'The' Civil War, as if it was the one and only, in fact there have been quite a few incivilities between the peoples of our green and pleasant land.

An earlier civil war, called The Anarchy, lasted for nineteen years, from 1135 until 1154. In that conflagration there were two people vying for the title of monarch: Matilda, the daughter of King Henry I, and her cousin, Stephen of Blois.

Another unneighbourly punch-up was The Wars of the Roses. This one lasted even longer, from 1455 until the death of King Richard III in 1485, although there were skirmishes beforehand and also flare-ups in subsequent years. Again, it was all about who wanted to be king!

A sleepy autumn day in Cheriton

So much for 'love thy neighbour!'

But let's get back to the fun in the middle of the seventeenth century. Billions of words have been written about the English Civil War, so to sum it up in a few dozen is nigh on impossible. But here goes...

We all probably learned at school that the English Civil War was a conflict between the Monarch and the Parliamentarians. As with any protest group, those who join inevitably have their own issues and so the agenda becomes more and more unwieldy, which is what happened with the cause of the 'Roundheads'. Perhaps the main issues were about the power of the king; the power of Parliament; the rights of the ordinary men of England; and how God best liked to be worshipped.

Your view may well have been influenced by that of your teacher. And yes, people today do still take sides about this war. Therefore, the pupils may well reflect the views they learnt in the classroom. Indeed, every teacher would like to think that this is so – if they never influence their pupils, it would be most disheartening!

It was an uncompromising king, Charles I, who believed in a God-given right to rule, which meant that his wishes and actions were the will of God. He was supported by the nobility and those who believed in the Divine Right of Kings, and their followers.

Against him and his faction (aided by those who supported their local lord) were the 'common' people, those who supported the House of Commons. In mediaeval times, this had meant the knights and burgesses who were chosen as representatives, rather than the nobles and high clergy who sat in the House of Lords. So, these 'common'

Reflections

people came from all ranks of society who, with equal fervour, believed that the King did not channel the will of God, and that the will of the people was paramount in good governance.

We will have learnt about battles: Edge Hill, Naseby – where the strength of the Royalists collapsed beneath the organised skills of the New Model Army as the war turned in favour of the Parliamentarians. Although there had been paid soldiers – mercenaries – in previous battles and wars, this was the beginning of our armed forces today: men trained to do the job, and commanders more likely to be selected for their ability rather than for the accident of their birth into the nobility.

What we were less likely to have been taught was the human tragedy – death or mutilation of the fighting men to a degree we might consider unimaginable in the days before modern warfare.

We are conscious of the terrible loss of life in the First World War. Family tragedies are still spoken of and, with the development of photography and film, images can haunt our understanding. The fighting population of England and Wales suffered losses of about one million in that conflict.

However, over the nine years of the Civil War, losses are estimated at around 100,000 fighting men from England and Wales. As the population of the country was just a fraction of that of the early 20th century, as a percentage it was far more devastating. Whereas the First World War lost 2.4% from a population of forty-two million, estimates of the English Civil War fatalities vary between 4% and 10% from a population of just seven million.

One of the more compassionate points about the English Civil War was an Act of Parliament from 1642. It recognised a 'duty of care' towards soldiers killed or injured and also towards the widows and orphans created by the conflict.

Although it was unlikely to have benefitted many of those in the conflict at Cheriton, the first military hospital – at the Savoy – was established in London which, along with two subsequent establishments, continued during the Interregnum. Nurses to care for the patients were recruited from widows, which predates Florence Nightingale by over two hundred years!

With the Restoration (of the monarchy), these hospitals were closed.

Off the beaten track: a reminder of turbulent times

Those losses of life also reflected a different sort of tragedy. It was a war of ideology, not a conquest of territory as so many previous wars had been. Not just against strangers, but neighbour against neighbour, between father and son, brother against brother. Families and friendships were fractured.

The early battles of the English Civil War had been predominantly Royalist victories, but by the time of the Battle of Cheriton, on the 29th March 1644, the Parliamentarians were in the ascendant.

The estimated numbers of soldiers in the armies at Cheriton do really show which side would have been the best one on which to put your money! Whereas the Parliamentarians could muster around 10,000 men, the Royalists could only manage half of this. By the end of the day the Parliamentarians were triumphant, and had lost about sixty of their men. The Royalists had suffered around three hundred fatalities. That's 0.6% of the Parliamentarians against 6% of the Royalists.

An example of how friend clashing against friend affected the adversaries even at the very top, Lord Hopton, leader of the Royalists at Cheriton, had been a good friend of the Parliamentarian chief commander, Sir William Waller.

Back now to the battle itself. The overnight advantage held by the Royalists was lost as Waller's men progressed to Cherition Wood. Hopton fought back. Whereas the Parliamentarians had a code of discipline, the Royalist chain of command broke down – overhasty behaviour by one group of combatants again gave the advantage to the Parliamentarians. Despite further attacks by the Royalists, they were continually rebuffed and by evening they retreated to Basing House.

Coincidentally, one of the leaders of a group of the Royalists was Sir Edward Stawell, probably an ancestor of Mary and Honoria from the following century at nearby Hinton Ampner.

Also on the Royalists' side was Sir Richard Tichborne, a member of the family we met earlier. Another member of the Tichborne family, Sir Benjamin Tichborne, was a signatory on the death warrant of Charles I in 1649, illustrating the way families were torn asunder by the conflict of the Civil War.

The Battle of Cheriton was a strategic victory for the Parliamentarians, as it had been their first offensive battle rather than defensive. It was also of key importance as it stopped the Royalist advance in the South and, consequently, any hope of a direct attack on London was vanquished.

"The pity of war and the pity war distilled" ('Strange Meeting' by Wilfred Owen) is reflected in the consequences for the ordinary people following a battle. Not only were there the deaths and terrible injuries of those who had participated, land and crops were destroyed, lawlessness – including the plunder of goods and livestock – left hardships that particularly affected the poor. Property was damaged or razed to the ground.

With the importance of the Battle of Cheriton in the progress of the Civil War, it is strange that, in comparison with other battles, it has fallen into relative obscurity.

Well! That's just over one thousand words! Not bad really.

A remembrance of another war and other lives

Hinton Ampner

The house and gardens at Hinton Ampner are owned and run by the National Trust. Like most of their properties, it takes more than a few minutes to do it justice! Particularly if you take advantage of the tea-rooms in the stables. The present house was severely damaged by a fire in 1960 and could have become yet another of the many grander houses of England lost in the twentieth century. However, Ralph Dutton – the eighth Baron Sherborne and the last owner of the house – restored the property.

Despite its ups and downs, Hinton Ampner as it is today

This house was not the only grand building on this site. An earlier residence was built in Tudor times for the Stewkley family who occupied it for many generations and, if legend is true, continued their tenure long after their mortal remains had gone!

Hot Gossip!

The fourth Baron Sherborne came to Hinton Ampner after his marriage to Mary, the elder daughter of Sir Hugh Stewkley. The younger sister, Honoria, was also present. Following Mary's death in 1740, local gossip made the obvious conclusions! So rife were the rumours, it was believed that Honoria had given birth to a child and, to prevent scandal, the babe was murdered. It was particularly tragic, perhaps, as they did not realise that the cat was already out of the bag. The couple continued to live at the house until Edward died in 1754, followed shortly afterwards by his sister-in-law.

In the following years, the house was let. And this is when the story becomes fun!

Cold Fear!

In 1765 a couple from London – Mr and Mrs Ricketts – rented the property and moved in with their children and servants. Almost straight away, night times were disturbed. Five years passed (un)peacefully. Mr Ricketts was called away on business. And while the cat's away, the mice will play, as they say! The ghosts started to have a field day!

Even though Mrs Ricketts' brother visited to protect her and the children, doors slammed and spirits dragging heavy weights and chains made merry throughout the nocturnal hours. By moonlight, a gentleman looking surprisingly like the late Baron, could be seen standing alone!

Even in the heaviest summer downpour, the gardens are lovely

Knockings, bangings and rustling silk gowns continued and, indeed, got worse. Voices, including a shrill female, could be heard. A fight and pistol shot added to the cacophony. The family fled, taking their servants and all their possessions with them.

The agent decided to spend the night there, but he left long before dawn!

Although another family chose to rent the property, they too did not last long.

Empty, the house fell into a state of dereliction. It was demolished and a new house was built in 1790.

Spring is sprung!

When Mary Ricketts spent her sleepless time there, an elderly man had told her that the former fourth Baron Sherborne had asked him to board up a box for him that, he told him, contained treasure. While the house was being demolished, such a box was found. Its contents were the skeletal remains of a baby.

The new house was quieter, but even so an occasional spectral visitor was recorded. The fire of 1960, however, was believed to have cleansed the house of its manifestations. Strangely, though, the last owner – Lord Ralph Sherborne – died following a fall down the stairs. So did he fall or was he pushed? And by what?

Watering Hole?

The local pub is The Hinton Arms. In its grounds is a small pool which is one of the sources of the River Itchen, which makes its way through Alresford and the famous watercress beds and on to Winchester. It must be stated, however, that the river is fed by several springs, so more than one place can lay claim to being one of the sources of this river. Perhaps the best liquid to find here probably comes in a glass.

Bramdean

To see... heaven in a wild flower

<u>Auguries of Innocence</u>; Wm. Blake)

Although a little distant from our route, there are a few churches that may be worth the excursion. One of these is the Gypsy Church, also known as The Church in the Woods, on Bramdean Common. I think an OS map reference (SU6329) might be rather helpful here!

It's a tiny church, secreted within woodland, that was the brainchild of the Reverend Alfred Caesar Bishop, MA, who realised that there were people, often living sheltered in the woods, for whom church-going was not a realistic option.

Although contemporary fiction often shows the more comfortably-off as having little regard for the poor, and charitable good works being a matter personal image than true care, here in Bramdean we can see the other side of the coin. The local people, led by the example of the vicar and his wife, made provision for those on the borders of society to be able to worship without having to travel great distances and without having to neglect their livelihoods.

It was advantageous to have the church brought to the people, as they would have been reluctant to go into Bramdean itself for the services. After all, if you were a charcoal burner, your income could be jeopardised if your burning was left unsupervised for any length of time. Also, those caring for animals would have not wanted to be too far from their charges.

The church was built in 1883, and when the Reverend Bishop's widow, Frances Katherine, died ten years later, she endowed money to be held in trust to secure the church's future. That it's still there is a credit to her goodwill.

Not only is the location of our Church in the Wood surprising, the building itself is quite unusual. Although this style of church was not rare at the time, neglect and disuse means very few of these buildings survive.

If I use the phrases 'catalogue shopping' and 'flat-pack', it probably conjures up visions of what I suppose might tactfully be called modest, sensible lingerie for ladies and Fair Isle knitwear for the men in conjunction with furniture from a large, cheerfully yellow and blue warehouse.

Certainly, it seems strange to us these days to imagine the Victorians would have done the same. I was aware that clothing was often bought through catalogues in the nineteenth century. I didn't, however, think that buildings might be ordered by letter (not on-line shopping, though).

However, it seems there was a good trade in economical, quick-to-build churches. Once our Gypsy Church had arrived, it took only five days to erect (no, it didn't rise on the third day, so perhaps the workers were slacking). I presume they put out all the pieces onto the ground and counted the nuts and bolts – well, at least a woman would have done so.

An unexpected Victorian treasure...

It is a rich green colour on the outside and the structure is made of corrugated iron. Inside, it is clad in a gorgeous dark wood, making it feel warm and welcoming. The windows are not particularly large, because larger windows were more likely to break in the post (perhaps the franking machine would have finished them off). High up, however, at the east end, is a delightful stained glass window. It is fitted out with all you would expect in a church, including pews and a harmonium. There is also a minute bell tower for calling the people to church. However, a group of campanologists might feel rather redundant with just one bell.

The cost was seventy-five pounds, which these days would amount to a very insignificant bill of less than seven thousand pounds for a building that can seat a congregation of fifty. But just seventy-five pounds? I can easily spend that on just one sole (and I usually get two at a time, with no two-for-one bargain), whereas our church for the same cost could pick up fifty souls every service!

...which still holds regular services

As I said earlier, very few of these flat-pack churches can be found these days, and Bramdean's corrugated building could have fallen into neglect and been lost too, had it not been for the people of the village and those living nearby who have banded together to save the church on several occasions, most particularly in 1986. Then Jim Lovelock, the village bobby, led a campaign to stop its closure. One of the 'old-school' of village policeman, he was a respected member of the community, and is still held in high regard by those who remember his dedication to his responsibilities.

It is characters like the Victorian vicar and his wife who established the Church in the Woods, and the dedicated village-folk like Jim, who create the communities which give rural life the timelessness, providing us all with that warm glow.

The church still holds regular evensong services throughout the summer, on the second and fourth Sundays in the month, at three o'clock. The congregation is quite full of regulars, although visitors are made welcome. Of course, natural daylight is used, although on the rare occasions there is an evening service, it is by candlelight as there is no electricity in this isolated location.

The fairest flow'rs o' th' season...

<u>The Winter's Tale</u>; Wm. Shakespeare

I love my little garden in Kent, and I like to think that any visitors also get equal pleasure as they look around my flower-beds. I am also aware how much work it takes trying to keep things under control. However hard I work at it, there's always 'tapete zizania' (that's 'carpet of weeds' to you 'n' me) and the somewhat lumpy-bumpy lawn.

It is therefore with great admiration (and a little touch of personal shame) that I visit gardens where so much care and dedication has been given to the flower-beds, lawns, paths, veggi-patches and so much more!

Although I could (but don't) bravely stick up a sign at the front of my house inviting passers-by to drop in and make their judgements, there are many people who regularly do just that! They take it further by advertising these occasions, and people will travel many miles, knowing that they are in for a treat.

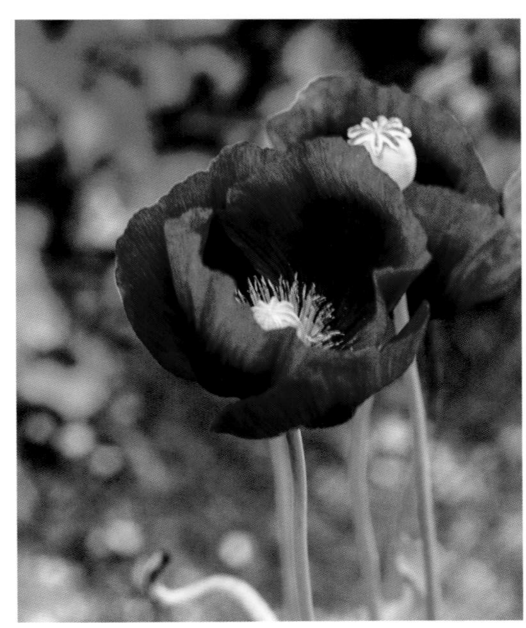

Flowers at Bramdean house flaunt themselves dramatically

Some will open their gates just once a year and others will do so more often, welcoming first-timers and recidivists who cannot resist a second or an umpteenth look around. By being part of the National Gardens Scheme, these dedicated gardeners have a chance to share their hard-work and design ideas with anyone who buys the little yellow book or goes on to the web-site.

Open at various times of the year, the scheme gives the visitor the chance to admire the spring flowers and the groundwork, including the hard landscaping, that will allow the later flowers to be seen at their best, and then to follow the year through to the season of mists and mellow fruitfulness. In Hampshire alone, more than one hundred gardens open their gates each year, some for just one occasion and others several times.

Fatal Attraction: a flower name to remember

Founded in 1927, the National Gardens Scheme has been promoting the gardens of ambitious amateurs through to professional plants-persons ever since. Visitors are asked to make a contribution upon entry, not to the gardener's personal mug-of-tea fund, but to some of our major charities. The majority of these foundations are part of the long fight against cancer, including the Macmillan Nurses, although other good causes are not neglected. About two and a half million pounds is given each year by the organisation.

Every flower enjoys the air it breathes

Lines Written in Early Spring; Wm. Wordsworth

Now, after that very long introduction, back to Bramdean and the big house, just to the west of the village, on the A272. If you are lucky enough, your visit will coincide with one of the open days, when you will have the chance to wander around the flowerbeds and lawns of this delightful garden.

First opened under the National Gardens Scheme in 1955, for sixty years now the gardens have been open to the public on half-a-dozen occasions each year.

Bramdean House's Open Garden Day: a wonderfully spent afternoon

It's a good job that the garden is large, because many people come along to these open days. In the summer it can easily be in the region of three hundred and fifty in just one day!

Many visitors are inclined to make a day of it, possibly with lunch in a country pub before exploring the paths, nooks and crannies at Bramdean House. Careful planning has resulted in delightful displays of annuals, perennials and shrubs in wide borders which appear to mirror each other.

Herbaceous borders and beds at Bramdean

For those with more specific interests and knowledge, there are extensive vegetable plots and trees (oriental cherries are in abundance, in a trial co-ordinated by the Royal Horticulture Society) and this year there have been trial-beds for a particular species, as part of a national project (I didn't know there are so many varieties of nerines).

Also, if you are a sweet-pea enthusiast, you will be in seventh heaven with the huge, enchanting array of these fragrant legumes! What is wonderful about these flowers is that, when you grow them in your garden, the more you pick, the more flowers will grow.

How does the little busy bee
Improve each shining hour . . .

<u>Against Idleness and Mischief</u>; Isaac Watts

As well as the planting, there is a delightful apple-house at one end of the gardens and also there are bees to keep the gardens flourishing.

Beehives beside the apple-house

Finally, if you feel our English country gardens need defending, you can join the children in a box-hedge castle!

About Turn!

If you have whiled away some time at Bramdean, then you may be wanting to redirect your steps towards to the South Downs Way. By retracing your path towards Cheriton, you can then continue a little further to the West and back to where you left the route, turning Southwards, and then you are on your way!

"Isn't that the path we should be on?"
HL

There is an alternative path back to the South Downs Way, so it depends on whether you are exploring the area or if your target is to complete the whole route of the South Downs Way. By retracing your detour as far as Hinton Ampner, you can turn South onto the Wayfarers' Walk, just to the East of the estate. It will bisect the South Downs Way about three quarters of a mile beyond The Milbury's public house. Having visited Hinton Ampner, a stroll through the grounds will allow you to join the Wayfarers' Walk without the need to go back to the main road. It is a good path and clearly marked.

The Wayfarers' Walk will lead you though the village of Kilmeston, nearby the church, and on the opposite side of the road is the Manor House, screened by a wall and tall trees and shrubs.

This private house was once owned by the Lacy or Lacie family, for 160 years, until 1739. Unfortunately, they do not appear to have been ancestors of mine!

Kilmeston Manor: one of the oldest manor houses in Hampshire

That's the Spirit!

The building is one of the oldest manor houses in Hampshire so, with such a long history, it comes as no surprise it's yet another spooky house. Unlike the old Hinton Ampner's phantom, the presence here seems to have more goodwill.

Remarkably, the hauntings do not appear to be connected to the remains of a Cavalier, wedged upright behind the panelling beside an upstairs fireplace. He was discovered in the 1920s and presumably had escaped Waller's Roundheads at the Battle of Cheriton almost three hundred years earlier.

Here at Kilmeston, our Grey Lady seems more than just benign, she is a domestic goddess! Believed to be a former loyal employee, even death did not make her hang up her apron. She tidies up, sorts out guests' belongings and turns down the bedding before it's lights out.

Now: a ghost that does housework? We'd all love one of those!

But Let's Drift Onwards

Now, having followed the Wayfarers' Walk Southwards, you will hardly have re-joined the South Downs Way before the opportunity for another diversion presents itself. The Monarch's Way branches off to your right, heading South. A short distance further on the South Downs Way will enable you to pick up the Wayfarers' Walk, again towards the South, should you wish to do so. Alternatively, you may wish to retrace your steps back to where you left the official walk.

Dean House, also in the village of Kilmeston, is another garden open to the public under the National Gardens Scheme. Truly magnificent, it is extremely popular with visitors. Perhaps 'shoes' and 'potato peeler' will arouse your curiosity enough to ensure a visit! (Pictures kindly provided by Dean House and Julian Blackwell)

Preshaw

Having seen several signposts to Preshaw and read about the Victorian barn which had been converted into a small chapel for the family who had lived in the 'big house', I was disappointed: like many such big houses it had fallen into disrepair as the family's generations suffered from the only two certainties in life: death and taxes.

Now the area is privately owned and the house has been restored into several apartments. So, despite those numerous signposts you have probably seen, at least as far off as the A272, suggesting that it is accessible (like any other signposted village), it is a quiet place where the residents appreciate their tranquil, private lives!

These Boots are Made for Walking...

This may be the time to mention some of the other footpaths that criss-cross this part of Hampshire.

In this particular area are the Wayfarers' Walk and the Monarch's Way, as you will have just read, but you may also be aware of – among others – the Pilgrims' Way and St Swithun's Way, both of which are back towards Winchester, and the Shipwrights' Way, nearer to Hampshire's border with West Sussex.

These paths vary in length from the easily manageable St Swithun's Way, at just thirty-four miles, to the incredibly long Monarch's Way, at over six hundred miles, of which I imagine most people would dip in and out. Otherwise, you'd need to put by a thirty-one day month and walk for twenty miles each day. Quite an achievement!

In between, there is the Shipwrights' Way at about fifty miles and the Wayfarers' Walk at more or less seventy miles. The Pilgrims' Way is a hundred and thirty-three miles - but that is really linking together the St Swithun's Way with variations on a sizable part of the North Downs Way in Kent. Looking at the various sites on the internet, I think that most of these measurements were done with a piece of elastic, as so many different distances are given!

Of the five paths, the Monarch's Way and Pilgrims' Way have historical roots and routes. You might think that the St Swithun's Way and the Shipwrights' Way do as well, but they are both created from someone's imagination – not that there's anything wrong in that – one from an historical character and the other a hypothetical trading route. Both have been devised to traverse attractive landscapes, and the Shipwrights' Way was conceived with cyclists in mind. The Wayfarers' Walk appears to be linking a range of footpaths, perhaps drovers' roads or public footpaths, and a memorial to a pioneering aviator. And also rabbits.

Saints

The Pilgrims' Way, although an ancient journey, is also the link for two other paths. Loosely, it is the route taken by pilgrims in mediaeval times from Winchester to Canterbury in Kent. So it begins with what is now the St Swithun's Way for the first thirty-four miles up to Fareham. After that, it more or less follows the path taken by the North Downs Way, through Surrey and Kent. Don't, however, get this confused with Geoffrey Chaucer's pilgrims in The Canterbury Tales, travelling from The Tabard Inn at Southwark in London towards Canterbury. They were roughly following the road we now know as the A2.

In fact, there were lots of pilgrim trails all over the country heading towards abbeys, monasteries and cathedrals all over the place that claimed to possess relics of the saints where people could get absolution (wipe the slate clean) for sins committed, or possibly be cured of an illness through the intercession of the saints with God.

Many of these relics were of a questionable nature – perhaps the knucklebone of a distant saint donated to a religious house, or a piece of the True Cross spirited from the Holy Land. At least Canterbury had its own in-house saint, Thomas Becket, who met a sticky end on Christmas Day, 1170.

The wealth of a religious house could, with the right saint, be stupendous. And much money maketh merry monks!

Today, the Pilgrims' Way meanders through lots of towns and villages that would also have been visited by many a mediaeval pilgrim, so there are churches aplenty to include for those passing through. Of course, for the mediaeval entrepreneur, there were opportunities, particularly if yet another dubious relic could be conjured up. Tacky tourist 'souvenirs' are nothing new!

Kings?

At this point on your journey along the South Downs Way the Monarch's Way crosses your path. This is one of the longest 'Walks' in the UK (there are lots of lists, and the distances given on these lists are not consistent, but the Celtic Way is a great deal longer and The South West Coastal Path seems similar in length to the Monarch's Way).

This path has been designed to approximate the escape route of Charles II after the Royalist defeat at the Battle of Worcester in 1651. And didn't our Merry Monarch go on a right gavotte around the country! You would have thought that he'd have made his way to the nearest port as quickly as possible. It would appear he was being harried by the victorious opposition and had to change his mind several times.

Nevertheless, I'm not sure his whole journey was a terrifying escape from his enemies, for when he got to Old Winchester Hill – I understand – he took time out for a bit of huntin' and shootin', as any gentleman would!

Judging by the footpath, initially he travelled North as far as Boscobel in Shropshire, but there he made a loop and took up a southerly route, cutting through Stratford-upon-Avon (it's a pity there was no theatre there for him to enjoy: he was the kind of chap who liked that sort of thing), and then he traversed the Cotswolds on to Bristol, before heading more or less South again and the coast at Charmouth in Dorset and then along to Bridport. Once more he sprung off, this time towards the East, arcing through Hampshire and Sussex to Shoreham-by-Sea, where he eventually boarded a ship for France, and went into exile for almost a decade.

For the twenty-first century walker, there is another diversion – an extra few miles further East, presumably so some shopping can be added to the journey in Brighton! I'm not sure Charles would have hung around at that point, though.

Having described this marathon of a path, there should, perhaps, be a question about the name of this trail.

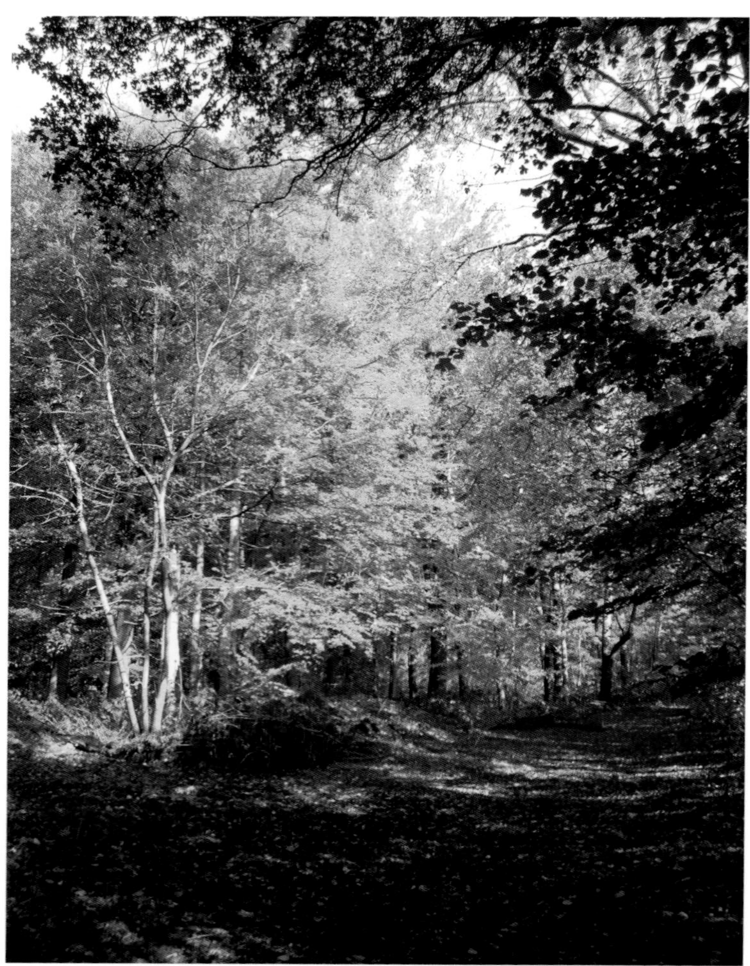

An Autumn stroll in the Hampshire Woodlands

At Cheriton, you may have questioned your allegiance towards the combatants in the Civil War. Your choice may well affect how you consider the name of The Monarch's Way. A Royalist supporter might say that his father – King Charles I – being dead, the royal title would immediately have passed to the heir presumptive so, from January 1649, Charles would technically have been the second of that name to be king, despite the coronation and anointing not taking place for many years.

A Parliamentarian would not have considered this accession to be so obvious. It would have made interesting reading in newspaper reports if a twenty first century journalist had time-travelled back to the mid seventeenth century: "the despotic leader of an autocratic dictatorship had been captured (in 1646). Arrested for crimes against the state, he was tried in a court of law, found guilty and was executed. His son, Charles Stuart, inherited the leadership of this discredited terrorist group and, following the defeat of the insurrection at Worcester, this traitor went on the run.

You can imagine our modern take on the story and why, perhaps, those with an affinity towards the Parliamentarians would disagree that the escape route used should be called the 'monarch's' way. During this time, the Parliamentarians called this state of affairs the Commonwealth or Protectorate, and those seated in Parliament governed rather than a king.

But, as it is said: history is written by the victors!

Having said that, after the Restoration of the Monarchy in 1660, the period between the two Charlies was known as the 'interregnum' by the Royalists, meaning 'the interval between the end of one sovereign's reign and the accession of the successor'. So, even in their eyes, it would be inconsistent to call Charles Stuart, son of Charles I, a "Monarch" in 1651!

Perhaps a modern Royalist might settle for "The Freedom-Fighter's Way"!

Boards!

When I read that the route of the Shipwrights' Way followed the imagined journey of a tree, I thought of the 'Scottish Play', when a wood goes walkies towards High Dunsinane Hill! This fifty-mile trail tracks a hypothetical oak tree on a hypothetical journey from a forest in North Hampshire to the Royal Navy's dockyard at Portsmouth.

It is estimated around a couple of thousand trees might be felled for the building of just one ship. The Mary Rose was built in 1510 using just six hundred...and look what happened to her!

The Shipwrights' Way was planned to lead through woodland and along good pathways, allowing access for walkers, cyclists and the disabled. Nevertheless, wheelchair users will find much of the route impractical. With the modern road network, some sections of the way are on roadway or close-by, but there are stretches on car and lorry-free paths, which makes it a great and safer experience for children and others for whom cycling on roads is not a good idea!

To help travellers find their way, there are twenty way-markers – modern sculptures – representing the landscape and history at their locations. The natter jack toad looks rather jolly and the shepherd's crown is rather grand. But the one that near to the South Downs Way at Buriton is a cheese snail (fortunately, I've never come across one of these on any cheese I've eaten). A viewpoint in the Queen Elizabeth Country Park, through which the South Downs Way goes, has a Hampshire Downs Sheep upon the sculpture there.

The South Downs Way hiker will cross the Shipwrights' Way at the Queen Elizabeth II Country Park, near Buriton, as you edge closer to the boundary with West Sussex. Although this path would be a diversion from the main route, it is somewhere you might like to return for a more relaxing break, perhaps with friends or family and – maybe – a bicycle or two!

Landscapes

The path you may have taken from Hinton Ampner to this point on the South Downs Way was on the Wayfarers' Walk. This path does not follow historical events or characters, nor does it fantasise about the journey of a chopped down tree. Its construct is more about giving a pleasant walk through a range of attractive landscapes, so unless it's raining so hard you've got your waterproof hood up, you should have an enjoyable time.

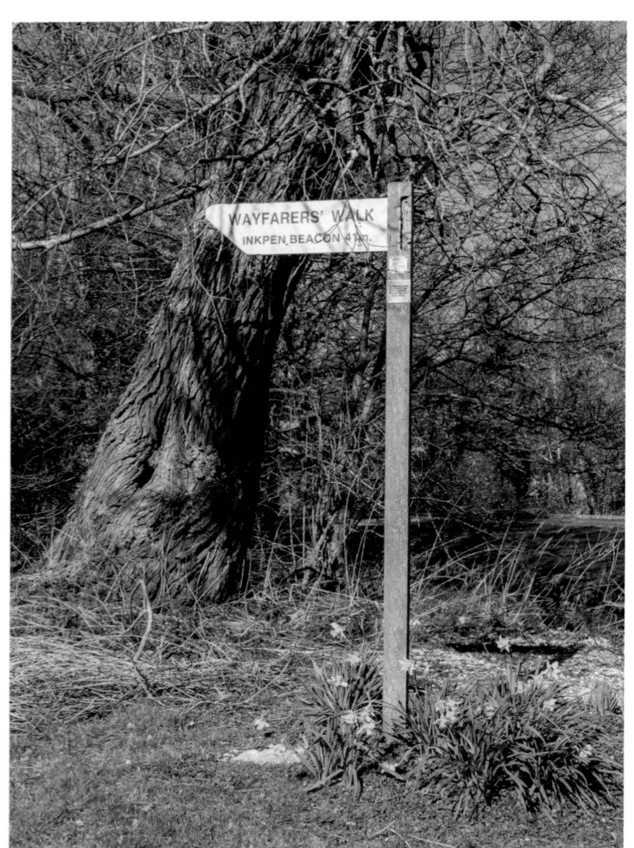

The primrose path of dalliance

The walk is approximately seventy miles long. Unlike the South Downs Way, the start and end points are not places 'of substance' merely a hill in Berkshire: Walbury, near Inkpen, and a T-junction with the Sussex Border Path, near Portsmouth.

The journey more or less follows a North/South direction. To a large extent it follows drovers' roads. These were long-serving tracks used by agricultural workers to move their sheep or cattle to fresh grazing land, or to shelter during the winter months, or off to market.

Along the way, the path skims Highclere Castle, an elegant stately pile. Often used for film and television productions, it has been the location of "Downton Abbey".

Not far onwards, there is a field called Watership Down, the setting for Richard Adams' story of Hazel, Fiver and their fellow rabbits gifted with psychic powers among their unrabbity talents.

Towards the A34, at Seven Barrows Field, is a memorial to Geoffrey de Havilland's first flight in his home made aeroplane in 1910. It is a strange place for the monument, as the successful flight actually took place at Newbury. Here at Seven Barrows Field is where an earlier failed attempt crashed in 1909! He went on to design aircraft like the Mosquito, which did its bit for King and Country in the Second World War. If the name de Havilland seems familiar, his cousin was the Hollywood actress Olivia de Havilland, and another cousin was also a Hollywood star: Joan Fontaine!

To get us back to our footpath, perhaps it's as well to say, as with the Shipwrights' Way, it is an area to return to for another day, another adventure.

Bawds!

The Wayfarers' Walk from Hinton Ampner follows the South Downs Way for a short way before branching off to the right, continuing its journey South. Less than a hand-span on your OS Map along this path is a location with a name to make you pause and, possibly, smirk – Betty Mundy's Bottom!

The derivation of this name is not clear – it may well be a dip in the landscape named after whoever owned it. There are explanations of the Romans calling it Beati Mundae, meaning 'the most blessed place in the world', which sounds almost as unexciting as the ownership bit.

However, legend has it that Betty was a girl in the time of the Napoleonic Wars with talents respected by both soldiers and sailors who were in need of some 'downtime' from their duties. Once she had offered to perk up their spirits, it is speculated that she lured them to this leafy hollow where her 'gang' stole the poor victims' cash, killed them and, with some sense of regulation, disposed of the remains. Nearby you will discover both Sailor's Wood and Sargeant's Copse. Make what you will of that!

Perhaps we should just stick to the South Downs Way, past the site of Lomer Village, deserted centuries ago, and make our way on towards Beacon Hill.

The approach to Betty Mundy's Bottom

Poo Bear?

No, I can't! I can't bear poo. If I say "poo bag", I am not talking about Pooh's mother but about the detritus left by inconsiderate, lazy dog-walkers.

Now, it is no defence to say the countryside is full of cow-poo, so why put the blame on poor pooches? Well, a cow eats grass – fibre – and a dog eats meat – protein. That means one smells far worse than the other. A cowpat is also good manure – enriching the soil, so a splat in a pat is just, well, messy.

Responsible dog owners know that what their pet leaves behind is a biological hazard that smells disgusting. Walkers who walk upright, head held high admiring the view, or stooped over a map feeling lost, often have the misfortune to plunge a boot in and, as a good boot has a deep tread, getting it clean is nigh-on impossible. This has the knock-on problem that a lunch-time pub break or getting into a car at the end of a walk becomes more than just antisocial.

So the responsible owner scoops up the offending pile into a small plastic bag and... then takes it home. What I really cannot bear is when these bags are left by the wayside, on fences or even lobbed up into the branches of a tree.

I hate to break the inconvenient news – there is no poo fairy to clear up after you and your dog. Don't pretend to yourself that you meant to pick it up on your return journey – you didn't.

People drop litter, they always have – that's thoughtless – but I'd rather see a sandwich wrapper or a discarded tin. Poo bags just turn my stomach. Environmentally aware folk will often pick up an old empty cake box, but they cannot be expected to take up a bacteria-enriched decaying poo bag into their clean hand just because some lazy irresponsible dog owners are so revolting.

So, thank you to those who are morally circumspect.

Right! I feel a lot better after that rant. Sadly, I know it will have no effect whatsoever upon the selfish and the lazy. Some will think I'm being faecetious about this, but lovers of the countryside will, I hope, be cheering!

Beauworth

For those who have continued on the route, there is a pub directly on the South Downs Way with an unusual feature that you may reach in time for your lunch-break.

Let's Raise a Glass (or Bucket)!

The seventeenth century inn, The Milbury's, is at the top of a chalk down that was, in times past, a Bronze Age barrow cemetery. This area of Hampshire has many other footpaths and many of them, as we have just seen, pass close by.

If you take water with your whiskey, you may need to take a walk!

If you venture further back into the building, past the bar, you will find a well, with its treadmill inside the pub! The well itself was dug out, before the days of machinery, to a depth of three hundred feet.

Nowadays, it is lit by electricity, although at the time of its construction candlelight was used and, along the way to the bottom, nails can still be seen that were used for hanging the candle as the workers delved. If you ask the landlord for an ice-cube, you can drop it through the grill and wait for a long time for it to hit the bottom. Alongside the well is the wheel that was used to raise the water to the surface.

Upon leaving the pub, the route continues along the road in an easterly direction for two thirds of a mile until it joins up with the Wayfarers' Walk where those who have explored the area may well link up again with our route on towards Beacon Hill.

Beacon Hill National Nature Reserve

Now, this hilltop is the Beacon Hill National Nature Reserve. Don't get too confused: there are quite a few Beacon Hills around, with at least two on the South Downs Way! This Beacon Hill is one of several places along the route that are areas where wildlife is protected (it's a Site of Special Scientific Interest).

It covers forty hectares (about a hundred acres) of chalk grassland and is an ideal spot to sit down with a flask of coffee and absorb the landscape, surrounded by wild flowers, birds and butterflies. Even on a late winter's afternoon, as the sun dips behind you, the views across the southern slopes towards Exton and beyond are delightful.

An Autumnal approach to Beacon Hill

Baa Baa Black Sheep!

There are probably lots of people who would only recognise a sheep if it looked like Shaun, from 'Wallace and Grommit'. Well, there are other breeds of sheep, and they can all look very different!

The Cumbrian Herdwick sheep

While strolling around Beacon Hill, I peered over a hummock and found myself eyeballing a Herdwick! Completely discombobulated, for a moment I thought I was in Cumbria – that's where they belong (I thought).

Now, I'm not a sheep-spotter: I don't go around with a little notebook recording what breeds I can see from a platform. But a Herdwick is very distinct. Yes, I agree, the South Downs should be covered with Shauns and their cousins, the Timmys. After all, if those two are not Suffolks, they could well be the Hampshire Downs breed.

Shaun's legs are rather like a ballerina's in black tights, whereas a Herdwick is sturdy – with legs more like Usain Bolt's in baggy white long-johns.

A Herdwick lamb

Surprisingly, these sheep are born totally black, taking two years to fade to their familiar grey body and white head and legs.

I think that part of their friendly appearance is that they seem to have a double smile – their mouths permanently giving a benign smile and their dark nostrils have the shape of a second: two for the price of one! So, a large sweet white face, with a cute smile, on top of a grey dreadlocked ball of wool, totally confused me.

This Lakeland breed nearly died out early in the twentieth century, but the author Beatrix Potter left money in her will to help to perpetuate the strain.

So, what are they doing on the South Downs? Well, these hardy characters are low-

maintenance, they are not fazed by the steepest hill or bad weather and they do not need rich pasture – they graze scrub and regrowth and other tough material. Just right to act as hillside lawnmowers maintaining the landscape of a nature reserve.

Although the fleece is of little value on the open market, the meat is lean and tasty with a strong flavour.

So, what's not to like? Well, it may be my imagination, but I've lost count of the number of times I've struggled up mountain paths, gasping and panting, to find my way blocked by a Herdwick, who baas loudly – and I'm always sure it is laughing at my hopelessness!

The path onwards to Exton: so easily missed if you're chatting too much!

Exton

Cometh the hour, cometh the... village!

The village of Exton has felt like my undoing! The curious story of the clock struck me so much that I came to a halt, as my investigations seemed to wind down. Alarm bells rung after a visit to the church...a mystery... had I hit upon a scandal? This became a 'hands-on' enquiry. My starting point was the wooden board, rather like a table-tennis bat, upon which I read information about the building: a man from the neighbourhood had given the people of Exton a prestigious gift of a clock which they had returned a couple of years later "the giver being disapproved of by the inhabitants".

However, firstly there are other interesting points in the church and village before I continue with this detective story.

We'll have the hags flung out ...in honour of the artist

Although St Peter's and St Paul's Church is from the thirteenth century, much of the interior design is part of the Arts and Crafts movement, the work of an architect and designer, Charles Spooner (1862–1938). He was a quiet, self-effacing man, which is a pity because he remains relatively unknown, whereas his cousin – William Archibald Spooner – is remembered for his verbal creations. 'Who?' you might say. Well, William has a word named after him: Spoonerisms. And what is one of those? It's where word beginnings get mixed up in a sentence.

Whether Cousin William did it by accident or just had a quick mind and a skill, we shall never know, but sentences like "The Lord is a shoving leopard" or (to one of his students) "You have hissed all my mystery lectures, and were caught fighting a liar in the quad. Having tasted two worms, you will leave by the next town drain!" have brought him everlasting fame.

However, let's get back to the church and Charles Spooner. He was a follower of the work of William Morris and this is reflected in his own designs. Many of his works were in churches, not the grand ones, but those in quieter, more rural locations. In fact, his choice of commissions reflects something of the man himself.

The glass, the wall-paintings and the furniture are all the work of Charles Spooner.

Nevertheless, it is remarkable that we know anything about the stencilled wall painting behind the altar.

The Arts and Crafts East window with 'The Tree of Life' wall painting by Charles Spooner

Only thirty years after completion, the wall paintings were decorated over in an attempt to repair a damp problem, and were then forgotten.

A redecoration of the church in 1995 struck problems when the new paint started peeling only weeks after its completion. The 'problem' was discovered to be the Arts and Crafts design of the 'Tree of Life'. Fortunately, it has now been restored.

The Strange Case of the Missing Clock

Although this title has a ring of Sherlock Holmes about it, I'm sad to say Sir Arthur never actually began a story with "The Strange Case Of... " What a pity! Robert Louis Stevenson's "Dr Jekyll and Mr Hyde" was a 'strange case', however. And here we seem to have a Member of Parliament (of course, an entirely respectable figure) with a somewhat darker side to his story.

The case began with that snippet of information in the church at Exton about the returning of the clock to the donor. Apparently, the parish had been given a clock in the 1830s which was erected with pride upon the church tower. Exton must have felt like its time had come! In an age when time was beginning to be no longer a local matter, Exton was ahead of the game the day that the MP for Salisbury had presented the villagers with a clock.

People out and about in the village on a sunny Saturday morning

Until the beginning of the railways, whatever o'clock it was was gauged by the position of the sun in the sky. At its zenith it was midday: as the sun progressed from East to West across the firmament, towns, cities and villages would judge the time at midday as it appeared to be where they were, so midday in London was earlier than in Bristol by ten minutes. Once railway timetables were devised, these variants meant that no-one really knew when the next train was due, rather like these days!

Thus it was in 1847 Railway Time was adopted by the rail companies, and in 1880 Greenwich Mean Time was officially adopted for mainland Britain, standardising the time from East to West across the whole country.

Despite being ahead of the crowd, the railway never did actually come to Exton. The route of the Meon Valley Line passed by about half a mile to the East, but even that was one of the last built to main-line standards to be opened – in 1903 – and it remained a passenger route for just over fifty years. But more of the great railway mystery in a moment!

Until that point, midday in Exton was the same as any other place on that line of Longitude, but not the same as anywhere else. Probably, for most farm workers, the times of the seasons were more important than worrying about whether the minutes and seconds were spot-on. So the presentation of a clock would have been a momentous occasion, announcing that this village was looking to the future.

To have a time-piece in the middle of a village in an era when not everyone had a watch must have been a matter of great satisfaction for the community.

The gentleman who presented the village with the clock was the MP for Salisbury, Wadham Wyndham (1773–1843). So far so good! However, as an observer from the future, I still can't help feeling it was a mightily strange thing for the MP for Salisbury to do, even if the family home was just up the road at Corhampton!

In the first place, why give the clock to Exton? Mr Wyndham was acknowledged in the press for his generosity in his constituency of Salisbury, particularly to the poor – for example, sums of one hundred guineas (a huge sum in those days) were given to charities at Christmas – but he would have had little to gain by such munificence towards a small village so far away from his voters!

Secondly, giving a clock seems so out of character when his usual offerings were financial. My suspicions are that it was an early example of 're-gifting': passing on an unwanted gift to someone else while pretending it was a thoughtfully selected present for the recipient.

Nevertheless, at the time the good folk of Exton were delighted! So delighted that the money to pay for it to be mounted on the wall of the church tower was raised by public subscription. Their pride was reflected in a painting of the magnificent clock upon the church tower, by the artist R H C Ubsdell

We have heard the chimes at midnight

Henry IV, part ii; Wm. Shakespeare

Strangely, in 1840 the villagers took down the clock and gave it back to him "the giver being disapproved by the inhabitants".

Exton's 13th Century flint church, St Peter and St Paul's, on a lovely day

Now, in this day and age it is easy to see how we might find issues to irk us about our elected representatives, so my initial thoughts about the actions of Mr Wyndham drifted towards duck houses and dog food – parliamentary expense claims that seem a little hard to justify. But these are not really issues to get so hot under the collar about that they would cause village worthies to go to all the bother of taking down a treasured clock and returning it!

My mind then wandered to the sort of scandals that have recently made headlines, resulting in criminal investigations and the censure of society. Well, these things certainly went on in times past, in fact so much so it was just seen as a fact of life by the poor (Tess, the eponymous heroine in Thomas Hardy's book is a prime example), but without supporting evidence, it may be as well to eliminate these from the case.

So, searches on the internet and at the Archive Department for Hampshire, in Winchester, kept me well and truly occupied...with very little success. The most interesting thing I could find out about Mr Wyndham and any local connection was that his gardener won second prize in the cucumber growing competition.

With the help of the staff at the Archive Department, however, a brief mention of the clock was found in the vestry records for Exton on 15th August, 1839: it would appear that despite their pleasure at the receipt of the clock and their willingness to club together for its installation, the villagers could not agree to pay for the "expense of winding up the clock and keeping it in repair."

It seems such a small point to fall out over, but I suppose that is how committees work! I still can't help but feel there must have been something more.

In an era when Parliament was introducing The Reform Act (changing how people voted for their representatives) and the introduction of various agricultural laws, there may have been more reasons to feel antipathy towards Wadham Wyndham.

It would also seem that he was on the board of a railway company that chose to change its plan for a railway line to Southampton to one which would go through his constituency of Salisbury, but it's unlikely this would have had any direct consequences for the people of Exton, although they may well have been rather miffed!

So, unless some more evidence can be unearthed, we are left with the fact that, although he was happy to give the villagers the clock, his goodwill ended there! And the people of Exton presumably saw the gift as an unwelcome burden.

A little learning is a dang'rous thing

An Essay on Criticism; Alexander Pope

Perhaps a warning about too much reading and study is a wise thing at this juncture! St Peter's and St Paul's church certainly provides this. Inside the church is a rather interesting grave stone. Grey and rather dour in appearance, it is all too easy to miss. However, notice should be taken, as the carving at the top gives a salutary warning: a man surrounded by his library of books is greeted by the Devil!

Too much of a good thing? The scholar gets his comeuppance

Outside in the church yard are five other unusual grave markers. They are simple but rather beautiful cast-iron examples. Although common in other parts of the country, for example Lincolnshire, they are quite rare in the South. The majority are from Victorian times up to the early part of the twentieth century. The dates on the ones here are all from the 1890s.

Rust in peace!

It has been mooted that iron grave-markers were cheaper to make than the traditional stone version, so some were obviously used for economy. Those made of cast iron are quite durable, whereas those of wrought iron are less likely to have survived. Some more elaborate ones were obviously more costly and were either made for a bit of post-mortality one-upmanship or as an artistic statement. With the village smithy just down the road, next to the present location of The Shoe Inn, they might well be examples of local craftsmanship.

In the garden of a nearby cottage is a garden seat made entirely of horse-shoes, again most likely from the local smithy!

Just Shoo-In to The Shoe Inn

No-one seems sure why Exton's pub has this unusual name. There seems to be no connection with cobblers, but with the farrier in such close proximity it may well be the simple explanation for this, and also for the name of the lane (Shoe Lane) in which they both stand.

The pub has not been in its present location for eons, however. The old flint building was on the other side of the road, beside the river, in what is now the pub's garden. Eventually, there was one flood too many, so the old pub was flattened in the 1950s and its replacement was built on slightly higher ground. Bob, who has lived his whole life in Exton, recalls that, as a boy, his father carried him into the flooded pub and sat him down upon the bar while business continued around him as normal.

The Shoe Inn

The gateway leading to the old forge, next door

Corhampton

To the casual traveller, Corhampton and Meonstoke might appear to be one village, such is their closeness. It is rather like the front of your fleece: the zip up the middle being the River Meon that flows through the middle.

The River Meon gently flowing South through the villages

...and when the saints DON'T go marching in!

Corhampton is a small village just down the A32 from Exton, with a church called "Corhampton Church": surprisingly, unlike most churches, it appears to have always been named after its location and not after a saint or two. It is a late Saxon building which is in a delightful location, or perhaps it was in the days before heavy traffic on the nearby road. However, once you are in the heavily screened churchyard, it is possible – to a degree – to ignore the traffic.

At times like this it is possible to ignore the twenty first century rushing by on the other side of Corhampton Church

It is hard to approach Corhampton Church without noticing the tree. Yes: it's that big thing to the right of the path – but if you did miss it, it might be a case of not seeing the tree for the wood! The trunk is so big you can't avoid focusing upon it and just maybe you didn't look up.

If you concentrate on the church's porch, maybe you won't see the massive tree trunk

This is a yew tree (Taxus baccata), a species that is supposed to be able to live for over a thousand years, and this one, I'm told, could be twice that age.

It could well be this longevity which has given yew trees their almost mythical reputation. To the Christians, their tenacious hold upon life, their ability to regrow, can be seen as a metaphor for the resurrection. Pre-Christian beliefs, for example Druidism, also held the tree to be sacred.

I suppose any tree which once it has been felled and used in a building can then sprout new shoots, would be considered quite magical.

So, that's one reason why we shouldn't be surprised to find them in churchyards. However, perhaps we should really be thinking either more humdrum or even gruesome!

The ancient gnarled wood seems to have faces looking at you as you pass

Firstly, in 1307, the king – Edward the First – decreed that yews should be planted in churchyards because the foliage is so dense it would protect the building against gales and storms. Perhaps it is as well that Leylandii were not around then, or we might be lumbered with them instead.

Secondly, tradition has it that yews thrive where there are corpses! So the question you need to ask yourself about why churchyards yews are generally bigger than woodland ones is – is it because they have the space and are not crowded out by other species or is it all the scrumptious underground nutrition?

Now, for years I thought that the yew trees were in the churchyards to supply the need for longbows, a most deadly weapon. The yew's flexible wood is what gives the bow the speed and power that justifies its reputation. It was the mastery of the English archers that gave King Henry V the upper hand at Agincourt. In William Shakespeare's play of that name, the tally of the dead gives us a good idea how the smaller army had annihilated its enemy:

This note doth tell me of ten thousand French
That in the field lie slain…
Where is the number of our English dead?
Edward the Duke of York, the Earl of Suffolk,
Sir Richard Kikely, Davy Gam, Esquire,
None else of name and of all other men
But five and twenty…

(Act 4; scene 8)

However, before we start the patriotic bonhomie, these figures are just a tad overblown. Yes the English army was the smaller, and yes the longbow played a not inconsiderable role, and yes it was the victorious side...and yes the dead were disproportionally French. Maybe it was around five thousand to about two hundred losses, and many of those French were slaughtered when Henry chose to kill the prisoners that they had taken, so perhaps we should avoid behaving like the FA Cup winning team's supporters when thinking about the English victory at Agincourt.

In mediaeval times all men were expected to practise this martial art! To supply the need for bows, yew trees were essential.

So, I'm forced to ask, if the yews were grown in churchyards to provide longbows, as we've long been told, and all of these men required weapons, how come there are any yews left anywhere in any churchyard? Perhaps it is quite the opposite – those in the churchyards, for spiritual or superstitious reasons or as a result of King Edward I's law to protect the buildings – were the ones that were saved from the axe!

Such was the pressure for more bows, demand exceeded supply. England ran out of available yew trees. We had to import them from Europe...and then it ran out of them too. The pressure was so great, in 1492 a law was passed that each ship importing goods had to bring in a quota of bows.

When Queen Elizabeth I commanded that firearms be used by the army rather than the longbow, she was actually insisting on the use of an inferior weapon, but that was because yew trees were so scarce.

So if the churchyard yews were – as we are so often told – there to provide timber for longbows, surely they would have been the first to go. Even if they had been planted as closely together as sardines in a tin, the churchyards would not have coped, and there would have been no yew trees in churchyards thereafter, let alone any boasting antiquity!

So I'd prefer to dismiss the longbow/churchyard story and to believe the yew at Corhampton is truly ancient. Even so, the heartwood is the first to die and decay, leaving wonderful hollows in the trunks. Arboriculturists point out that new yews can grow from suckers, so it is not easy to know a tree's age when its nativity is beyond recorded data.

Whatever its age, its dense foliage and stature provides a wonderful, fragrant shelter from the elements – a sudden torrential downpour would be screened by such a magnificent umbrella, which could transform itself into the sweetest of parasols against the burning heat of Apollo.

Perhaps these notes on this splendid tree, part of our English landscape, should be completed with another quotation by William Shakespeare, from 'Richard the Second', describing the deadliness of the yew – both its toxicity and as a weapon – in just one, hyphenated word: 'double-fatal'.

Clock This!

Before entering the church, step to one side of the porch and look slightly up at the South wall of the building.

There you will see a round stone carving with a hole in the middle. This is a Saxon sundial.

With this glimpse of sun, telling the time must be difficult!

Unlike modern ones, this is a case of 'bring your own stick'. To tell the time you would have needed to place your stick in the hole so that you could take a reading using the scored lines around it.

I have used the past tense here because whoever thought a porch would be a good idea has placed it so that, for much of the day, the sundial is in shadow! Perhaps the builder didn't worry because he thought that the clock was faulty, as the Saxons didn't have a twenty-four-hour day. So, you can't put your watch right by it anyway!

Cromwell or not Cromwell? That is the question

It is popularly maintained that the people of the Commonwealth under Oliver Cromwell were somewhat puritan in their beliefs, and held that the simplicity of their places of worship should echo the purity of their faith. To that end, the embellishment of the earlier churches with delightful wall paintings was considered an abomination.

However, to what degree can we hold Oliver Cromwell responsible for the destruction? Well, not much. The beginning of the damage had been done over a hundred years earlier.

One of the church's surviving wall paintings

This was in the time of Thomas Cromwell, Oliver's step-great-great-great-uncle, the son of a blacksmith from Fulham. Sharp intelligence and a keen knowledge of the ways of the world enabled him to rise to be chief advisor to King Henry VIII. Cromwell was an advocate of Protestantism, holding that – among other things – the Bible should be in a person's own language, not Latin, allowing them direct access to the word of God.

However, Thomas Cromwell sensibly decided to begin the cleansing with the monasteries in 1534. After all, the abuses of the rules of their orders had made them unpopular with the King's subjects and the wealth of the foundations would enrich the King's coffers! It was a win-win situation.

Largely, the churches did not suffer under the new doctrine of English Catholicism practised at this time. It was during the reign of King Edward VI, from 1547 to 1553, that the churches which had retained their pre-Reformation glister were targeted. Wall paintings were plastered, statuary was smashed and stained glass shattered (but the last of these only sometimes, as the cost of new glass – be it ever so plain – was so prohibitive only the most zealous reformers would go that far). When Queen Elizabeth I acceeded to the throne, the obliteration continued.

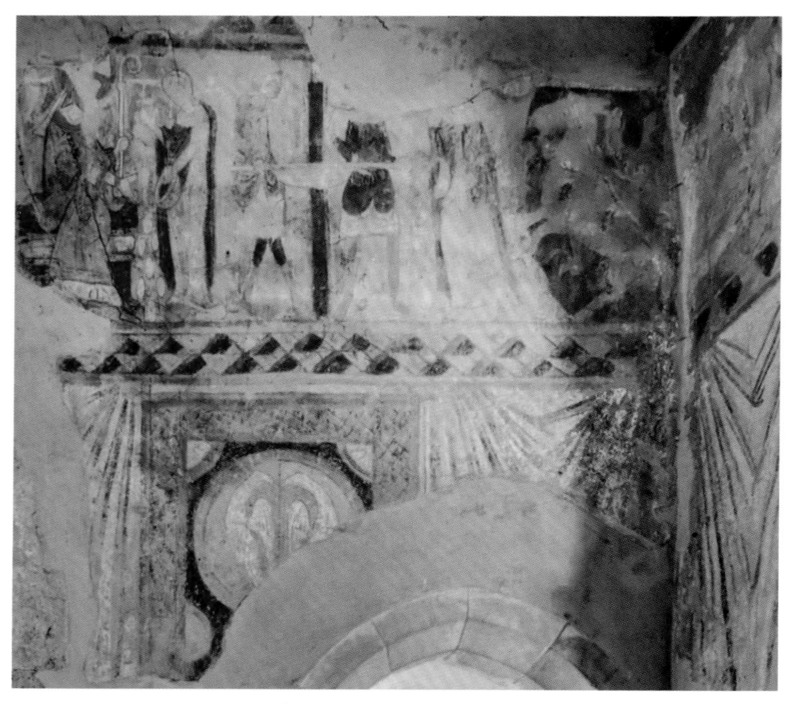

Another of the wall paintings

The simplicity of the interior has appealed to church goers over the centuries, especially those in the seventeenth century

Over the centuries, generations of worshippers would cease to know about what was hidden on the walls that surrounded them. Restoration and renovations in Victorian times sometimes revealed these hidden delights but their true worth has only fully been appreciated in the last half century. Perhaps the rise of holidays abroad, giving us the opportunity to see places of worship further afield, has increased our interest, and our desire to rediscover and preserve these images.

Does this mean that we can exonerate Oliver Cromwell from the damage to our churches and that we should put the blame on his ancestor? Well, again the answer is no. Despite the

destruction in Tudor times, there were still remnants of the mediaeval art work, so the Roundheads finished the job from the previous century, including taking the sparkle out of the remaining stained glass!

It is probably not unrealistic to be a little grateful to these reformers for their brutal elimination of the wall paintings. By covering them, they were protected and preserved for us to admire today.

Meonstoke

From Ancient Grudge Break to New Mutiny...

Romeo and Juliet; Wm. Shakespeare

My map showed so clearly how close together the churches in Corhampton and Meonstoke are, at a distance of about two hundred yards. Strangely, they are also miles apart!

Having noticed the people of Meonstoke were having a coffee morning in aid of charity, I took myself along to ask why these two communities, with only a river between them and linked by a bridge, needed two churches. "Well, we hate each other!" I was told by a lovely lady with a big smile.

A warm spring day encourages lichen and other life to thrive

Fortunately, she then went on to explain. When the Saxons and Jutes invaded the area – about one and a half thousand years ago – they had two encampments, one on either side of the river. These two groups had nothing in common and were at war with each other. The hostilities between the two communities continued for hundreds of years, which resulted in two churches and two groups of people who avoided each other as much as possible.

These days, hostilities are more like a good natured rivalry – thank goodness (otherwise I might have been forced to find another charity coffee morning and eat another huge piece of rather delicious chocolate cake, just to be fair).

Indeed, at the turn of the millennium, the church in Corhampton needed restoration and the two villages worked together to raise the one hundred and ten thousand

pounds needed for this. Then the people joined forces to raise a further quarter of a million pounds for Saint Andrew's Church in Meonstoke for its restoration. Although the English Heritage Lottery Fund chipped in, local people worked together with not only generous donations but also fund-raising events to raise the cash.

So, if you are passing through a village where there is an open garden to visit or a coffee morning, it is not an indulgence to eat cake: it is a necessity!

Although it is quite a small village, in its past Meonstoke must have been of some importance in the locality, as in the thirteenth century it was granted a weekly market and an annual fair, both requiring royal assent, and these would have attracted buyers and sellers from a wide area. Some other villages that attained such powers in the middle ages grew into the sizable towns and cities that we know today, so Meonstoke's wheel of fortune did not remain in the ascendant.

One of several interesting windows in the church at Meonstoke

Nestling behind The Buck's Head, you'll find this lovely church

It was this era that saw the building of St Andrew's Church, although there have been later alterations and additions.

The more you read, the more things you know

I Can Read with my eyes Shut!; Dr Seuss

Now, I have to confess that I was finding information on this village rather sparse, and so I took some time out to read an historic novel or two. Curled up in my favourite armchair, I was stunned to read the phrase "The manor of Meonstoke was acquired for me." (in 'The King's Concubine' by Anne O'Brien). So, I finished the chapter and started to look for more details.

At one time the village was known as Meonstoke Perrers, the addition being the name of the subject of my reading, and of the manor's most famous – or infamous – owner: Alice Perrers.

It would appear that she bought the manor, having been given the money from the Royal Exchequer by King Edward III, sometime after 1367.

Alice was, as far as we know, of lowly birth, but rose to became King Edward's mistress. The ignominy of her background meant her rise in royal circles, and the power and wealth that it gave to her, created dislike or even loathing among those with whom she mixed.

Her place in the royal household was offensive because Edward had had a long and successful marriage to his queen, Philippa of Hainault. For Edward to allow Alice to supplant his wife caused consternation. Edward had fathered at least twelve children with Philippa, nine of whom survived childhood (five were males, which was important for providing an heir), and so his behaviour was considered shocking and disloyal, and Alice was regarded as a wicked strumpet. She also managed to provide Edward with at least three more children!

However, after all those pregnancies and with failing health, Philippa was probably quite relieved to have someone else doing royal-bed-duty!

Following Philippa's death in 1369, Alice Perrers continued to warm the King's bed and stayed loyal to him in his declining years, until he died in the summer of 1377. As his mental faculties failed him, Alice's enemies were quick to exact revenge. Consequently, Meonstoke was confiscated (and then returned) on a couple of occasions, initially in 1376.

Eventually, in 1380, the manor was granted to Alice's husband, who sold it to the Bishop of Winchester, William Wykeham. This is a rather circuitous way of getting to the point about who owns it today – Wykeham then granted it to his own pet project, Winchester College, and it has remained in its possession ever since.

A Pane in the Glass (for backward-looking men)

In the early years of the twentieth century there were some repairs, including the insertion of an interesting window. It particularly caught my attention because it uses colours that I especially like – blues, purples and pinks. As you walk down the aisle, you will see it on your right. Made by Mary Lowndes, it is a memorial to Mary Laing, from 1906.

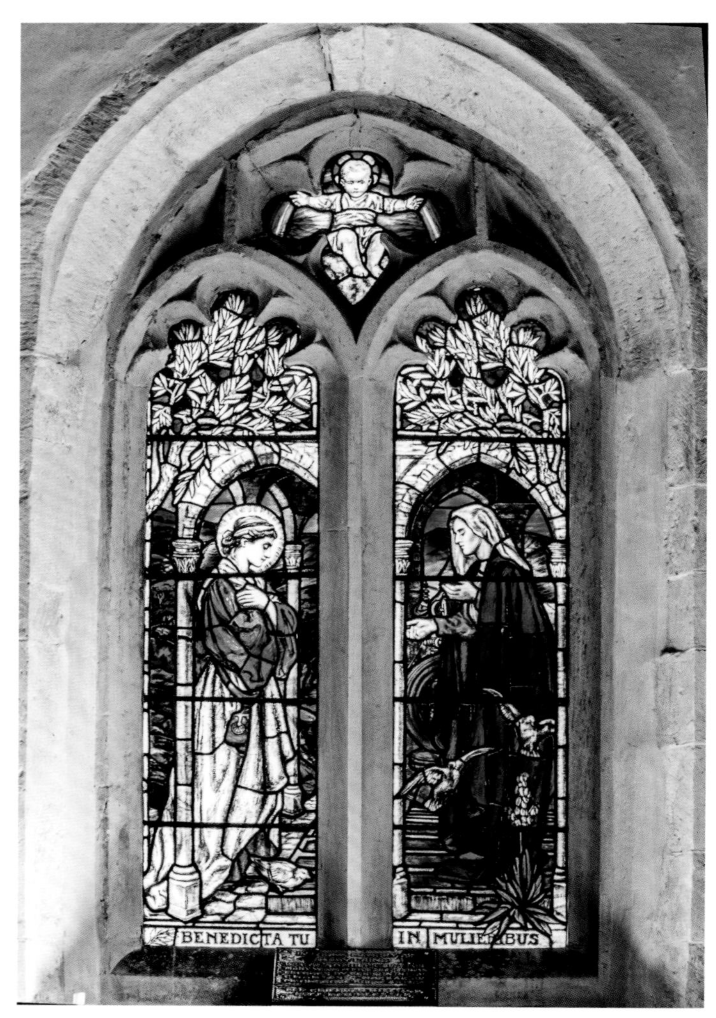

The memorial window to Mary Laing, from 1906

Mary Laing was the wife of Samuel, of Scottish birth, whose first contact with Hampshire was that his father sent him to school here. After Cambridge, he lead a varied career, from the Railway Board, as a Government official in India and as a Liberal MP in Scotland for a large part of the time between 1852 and 1887. As far as I am concerned, his contribution to life today is that he invented the third-class rail-fare (goodness knows what happened to second-class). So 'third-class' is the standard fare that most of us travel by these days.

Detail from the window created by Mary Lowndes: The Visitation: Mary meets Elizabeth

Samuel died almost a decade before Mary, so the memorial window was commissioned by her son-in-law, Charles McRae. Sadly, I cannot find anything about Mary, although it is to her credit that Charles considered her worth what must have been an expensive as well as beautiful memorial window. Like so many women in the past, her contribution is obfuscated by the deeds of the men!

The memorial's date of 1906 was the year that Mary Lowndes, the craftswoman commissioned to create the window, founded her own business, The Glass House, in Fulham – an unusual thing for a woman to do, in more than one way. Establishing her own business was progressive, and for a female to work in stained glass was unusual in a craft usually done by men. Her Art Nouveau creations won her many plaudits.

The daughter of a Canon at Salisbury Cathedral, she was born in 1857, in Sturminster Newton in Dorset, and just sixteen years later she was studying at the Slade School of Art. However, it was not until the 1890s that she taught herself the skill of glass painting to complement her designing. It was in 1897 that she first set up in business with Alfred Drury, employing a whole team of craftsmen, allowing freelance designers to use their services for their own creations. The thriving business was able to transfer to better, more spacious premises at The Glass House in 1906, a purpose-built workshop. Before her retirement in the early 1920s, Mary had created well over a hundred windows, including this beautiful example here in St Andrew's Church.

She is also remembered for her political life, as she was a leading light in the women's suffrage movement. Not only did her artistic skills come to the fore designing banners, posters and other artwork for the movement, as Chairman of the Artists' Suffrage League and a member of the committee for the London Society of Women's Suffrage, she also took a leading role in many of their activities.

She saw votes for women become a reality after World War One, as she lived until 1929, long enough to see the first woman Member of Parliament and for women to get equal voting rights to men in 1928.

So: Alice Perrers in the fourteenth century and Mary Lowndes more recently – both women who went against the conventions of their times and who have connections with this village.

ALICE PERRERS AT THE DEATHBED OF EDWARD III.
Alice Perrers at the deathbed of Edward III

And, perhaps, we should not forget Mary Laing, to whom the memorial window in the church is dedicated. Men's contributions to history are recorded for posterity while all too often the role of the women is neglected. Although, admittedly, some women were born to greatness, some achieved greatness and some had greatness thrust upon them, the married woman left 'at home' just got on with it, and her chances of being remembered are all too slim. She was the one who, in a large household would be responsible for its smooth running: managing the staff, the finances, the purchasing, the social events for her husband. In a more modest home, the wife would have similar duties, and while

Edward III tomb effigy – ©Copyright: Dean and Chapter of Westminster Abbey

her husband – perhaps – went off to more 'manly' activities, she would also be running a farm or a shop or some other family business. Somehow, she would have to fit in pregnancy, childbirth and childcare around her other tasks.

Whereas in the First World War death rates were 2.4 percent of the fighting men, their women folk left at home, only seeing their menfolk on leave, were at a far greater risk through childbirth. At the time when Mary Laing might have gone through pregnancy, the maternal fatality rate was at least 5.5 percent.

So, really it is three women in Meonstoke who should be remembered, with Mary Laing as a representative of so many others.

Droxford

Droxford may seem a little far down the Meon Valley for those on the South Downs Way, but this sleepy village of around six hundred people is worth including here for a small but vital incident in the Second World War, as well as for a two of its residents, one from before that conflict and another from afterwards.

The First World War saw the First Battle of the Falklands when the Royal Navy swatted a more powerful German fleet under Admiral Grat von Spee, getting its own back after the Battle of Coronel.

Pretty cottages in the village of Droxford

The British commander in these reprisals was Vice-Admiral Sir Frederick Sturdee who lived in the centre of the village, and he received a hero's welcome from the locals upon his return home. It was Sturdee who, in retirement, saved Nelson's Flagship HMS Victory (more of this ship later) from being scrapped, and initiated its restoration and on-going preservation in Portsmouth.

Almost thirty years after the Second World War had ended, in 1974, a new rector was appointed to the village – the Reverend John Beaumont. During the Second World War he was quite a Houdini: after several escapes from German prisoner of war camps, he was sent to the notorious and allegedly escape-proof Colditz Castle. Pretending to be a Belgian, he became one of the elite who escaped, smeared in garlic inside a rubbish heap. I'm not sure whether the garlic was part of the disguise or if it was just bad luck that there was an extraordinary amount of the stuff in the rubbish! The really bad luck was that he was recaptured by the Germans who just happened to be on the lookout for a real Belgian!

And just to throw in a little by-the-way, a previous rector in the village was the husband of Izaak Walton's daughter. This famous fisherman, author of 'The Compleat Angler', spent his declining years here, whiling away his time, rod in hand, by the River Meon.

Meanwhile, back in Blighty, Droxford had its moment of glory. I would say that it had its fifteen minutes of fame, but it was forty-eight hours, and with the cloak of secrecy the fame bit didn't happen! As you will have read earlier, in 1944 the Allied troops were camouflaged all over southern England, awaiting the invasion of France.

Amid the waiting forces at the beginning of June that year, the tranquil village of Droxford had the spotlight of history upon it.

At the time the war leaders posed for this photograph it was supposed to be at Droxford. Railway boffins have identified the station actually to be Alton. (Crown copyright)

Almost twenty years later, in 1963, a discussion about what had happened to a picture that had hung in the waiting room at Droxford Railway Station (by then closed), started an enquiry which revealed a tiny but significant nugget of history!

Careless Talk Costs Lives

I do enjoy a bit of gossip! That's why I am staggered by the way that people did their bit for the war effort by keeping mum: not saying anything that might be secret.

Even after the Second World War was long over, many ordinary people kept 'shtoom' about places and events, even though such knowledge would no longer be a risk to national security. It was years before the Cabinet War Rooms in London were common knowledge. Likewise, the tunnels at Dover Castle were a matter of national security, and the code and cypher breakers at Bletchley Park – which would have dealt with information gathered by the Royal Navy at HMS Mercury, near to East Meon – revealed nothing until recent years. Since those secrets have come out, there have been documentaries and films, sometimes with more than a dash of fiction thrown in.

The Beginning of the End

Winston Churchill, 10th November, 1942

So, the happenings at Droxford in 1944 are also not everyday knowledge. Here it was that the leaders of the Allied Nations met at the beginning of June that year to discuss the final details of Operation Overlord – the Normandy Landings. Most of the hard work had been done, but this military operation was so important, last minute checks were a good idea. As they say: 'the Devil is in the detail'!

A photograph of the leaders, supposedly at Droxford Railway Station, was in common circulation not long afterwards – it was good propaganda to see our great and good in unity and friendship. However, those who know about railway stations, having looked at the background canopy above the platform, were convinced it was a set-up: it was not Droxford Station! More than likely it was Alton Station – what detective work by the enthusiasts!

So, without photographic evidence, how can we verify the story that Droxford was a vital location in military history?

The signalman at Droxford, Reg Gould, was tracked down at Botley. It was he who pointed local journalist Tim King in the direction of a retired Southern Railway manager at Keyhaven who, in 1944, had been tasked with finding a quiet location for eight railway carriages (Winston Churchill's personal war-time train, codenamed Rugged) which could not be seen from overhead.

A siding at Droxford came to mind, so this gentleman, a Mr Charles Anderson, was charged with shunting the train into this siding and sorting out telecommunications systems. Tim King resolved the mystery of the photograph: the real picture of the meeting had been given to Charles Anderson, MBE, upon his retirement! It is now in the National Archives.

Despite all the secrecy, the villagers were aware that something was going on, even if they didn't know what. Only recently, a local lady recalled that as a child she had peered curiously over the parapet of the nearby bridge and was shooed away by armed guards.

So, who was present? Surprisingly, Ike (General Dwight D Eisenhower) was not there – despite Hollywood giving the impression that the Americans did everything all by themselves. He was further along the way at his HQ, Southwick House – HMS Dryad – keeping busy.

Those who were on the train were Anthony Eden, Foreign Secretary; Ernest Bevin, Minister for Labour; Jan Smuts, South Africa's Prime Minister; (and also possibly Mackenzie King and Peter Fraser, the Prime Ministers of Canada and New Zealand) and of course Winnie was there!

Churchill's restored carriage, now in Derbyshire (Courtesy of The Princess Royal Class Locomotive Trust, in Ripley, Derbyshire, DE5 3QZ)

To be honest, even our Prime Minister's attendance was seen as unnecessary and likely to draw Nazi attention away from East Kent, towards where the really important stuff was going on – Hampshire.

The Trust has styled the carriage to the 1940s and showed how it was likely to have looked when Winston Churchill was in Droxford (Courtesy as above)

But at least it meant that Churchill's guests could enjoy a rather lavish dinner on the train, on 3rd June, as his personal dining habits do not appear to have suffered from rationing.

All in Good Friendship

Winston Churchill, 6th June, 1944

An even less-welcome participant was the leader of the Free French, General Charles de Gaulle. With France occupied by the Nazis, there were concerns that he might blow the gaff, particularly as things have never been tickety-boo between our two nations since the Hundred Years War.

So, when de Gaulle arrived at Droxford, he was pointed in the direction of the railway carriage, some 250 yards away, and forced to 'walk the line'. Churchill did not demean himself by walking down the line to meet him.

The entente cordiale did not improve after the war ended. The new economic alliance – the Common Market – was formed on mainland Europe and Britain wanted in, but de Gaulle would have none of it. It was three years after the death of de Gaul before the United Kingdom was admitted, and the squabbling has continued ever since!

Before Winston Churchill died in 1965, he had arranged that, following his state funeral, his coffin would be taken for burial to Bladon, near to his family home of Blenheim Palace in Oxfordshire. Logically, the train should have departed from Paddington Station, but Churchill had arranged that it should depart from Waterloo Station on the opposite side of the capital, as a final victory salute to de Gaulle!

We (or rather 'I') Shall Fight on the Beaches

Winston Churchill, 4th June, 1940

But back to Droxford and the go-ahead for the D-Day Landings. The villagers believed that the Allies, including Eisenhower, had made the decision to delay D-Day for twenty-four hours because of rough weather, until 6th June, in that train. However, as Eisenhower was not there, that cannot have been the true course of events.

So where was that decision made? Tim King put that point to ex-President Eisenhower in an exclusive interview when he visited Portmouth Guildhall in August, 1963. "Right there, in Southwick House, on the 4th!" was the reply. Tim did not expect an 'exclusive' with Ike: he merely strolled past a room with an open door and noticed the guest of honour inside and alone. And no good reporter likes to miss an opportunity – so he slipped inside for a chat! Can you imagine that happening these days?

This poses the question: why did Churchill want to be on the spot at this moment of history? Cabinet papers show that Churchill (who had done his bit on the battle-field during the Boer War) was as keen as mustard to be 'hands-on' at the Normandy Beaches. He obviously knew his 'Henry V' and all about leading his men into battle.

He had pulled strings so that he could travel over on HMS Belfast and then be there with the troops at Normandy. This ambition resulted in messages and phone calls flashing to and from the siding, his obstinacy eventually dragging King George VI into the fray. When the King found out, he was furious – the Prime Minister could not risk life and limb on such an expedition. So, he insisted that he would go as well: it would be both men or neither!

The risk of potentially leaving Britain with no Prime Minister or King at a stroke meant that Churchill had to back down.

Incidentally, the last British king to lead his troops into battle was George II, at the Battle of Dettingen in 1743. How differently might our modern history have been if the two boys had had their way!

Journalist Tim King relaxing on a bench of the former siding where the carriage stopped

Nowadays, with the Meon Valley Railway line just a distant memory and Droxford Station now a private

house, the location of where the meeting took place is in many ways even more of a secret than it was in the middle of the last century. With no railway tracks to be seen on what is now a very pleasant country walk, the Meon Valley Trail (which is approximately ten miles long) has an air of peace and tranquillity belying its past. To those who know, it is a glimmer into that moment in history which began the great push into Europe, but many people who stroll right past this historic spot, even sitting a while on a conveniently placed bench – right by the siding – to contemplate life and nature, are unaware of its significance in the history of our nation.

DROXFORD STATION
In a special train at this station, the
Rt.Hon. Sir Winston Churchill MP
then Prime Minister of the UK spent
some days making crucial decisions
with his staff prior to the
invasion of Europe on
D Day 6th June 1944

Just off the B2150 at Brockbridge a discreet sign on a letterbox shows the way to the railway siding

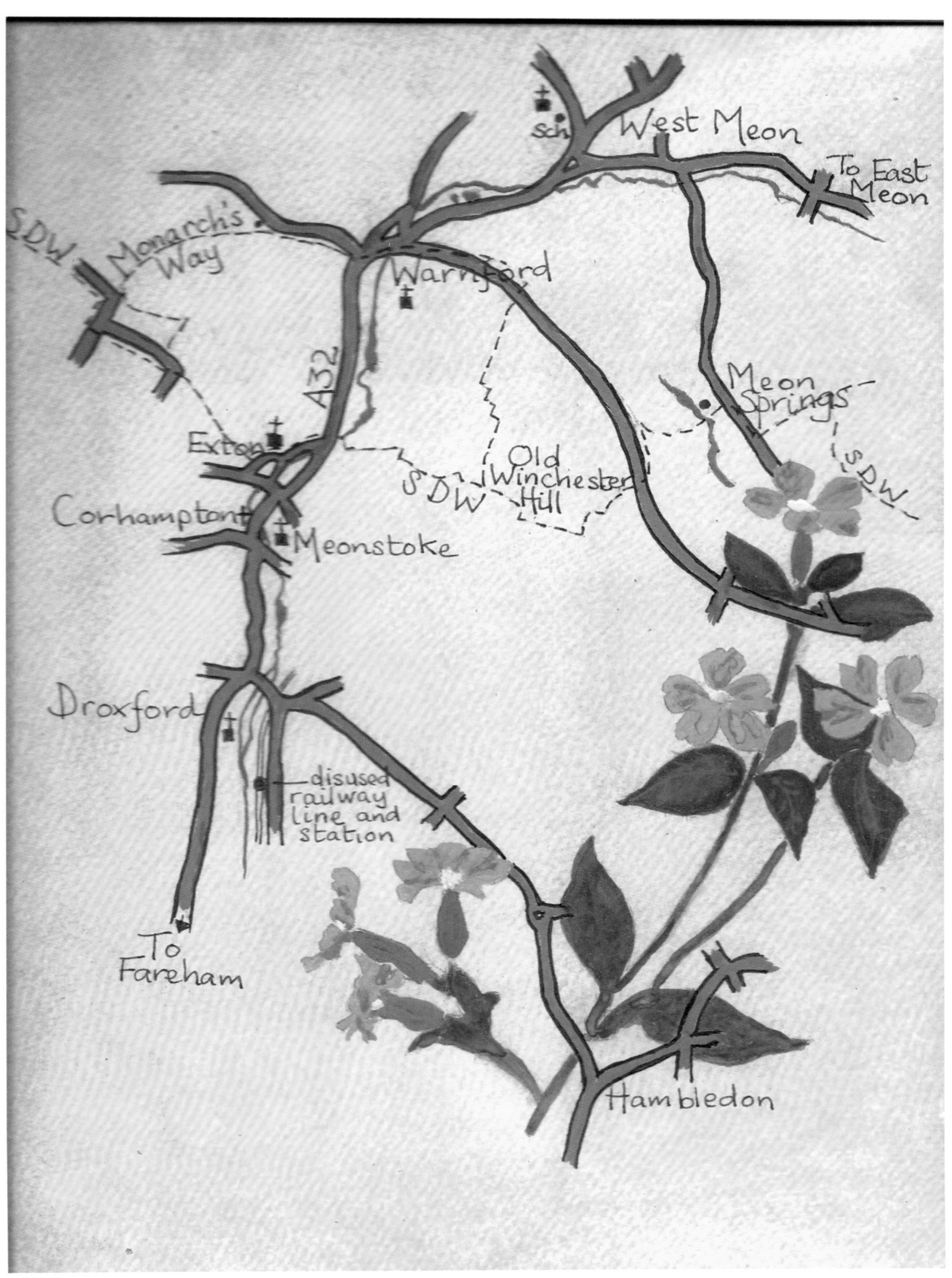

sch
West Meon
To East Meon
SDW
Monarch's Way
Warnford
A32
Meon Springs
Exton
Old Winchester Hill
SDW
SDW
Corhampton
Meonstoke
Droxford
disused railway line and station
To Fareham
Hambledon

Warnford

A Crafty Diversion

Although Hampshire has its public art – for example in Winchester there is the Anthony Gormley sculpure in the Cathedral as well as various works by Elizabeth Frink around the city, and along the Shipwrights' Way there are some interesting way-markers representing the history and landscape – it is good to see that the county has its own craftsmen and women producing exciting work.

Just to the west of the A32 at Warnford, there is a prime example in the work of Charles Normandale at Wheely Down Forge, an artistic blacksmith. Although the South Downs Way does not pass immediately by the forge, the Monarch's Way provides a link between our main route and the forge.

Jaws?

As you pass by, in the field to the side of the forge are some interesting pieces including, if my memory serves me well, a rather silly looking shark (and any shark in a field has just got to look rather absurd)!

In a career spanning more than forty years, the majority in his own business, Charles Normandale has developed a world-wide reputation and his work can be seen in many public buildings and open spaces.

In my home town in North Kent, for example, there are the glass screens and door to a chapel for private prayer in the crypt at Rochester Cathedral.

Many of us will have visions of the blacksmith at his forge: the roaring flames and the white-hot metal, along with the sounds of the hammering. In the bucolic dreams of the perfect village, one of the few sounds to be heard would be the ringing out of beaten metal on anvil, its sounds echoed in the work of composers like Wagner and Verdi.

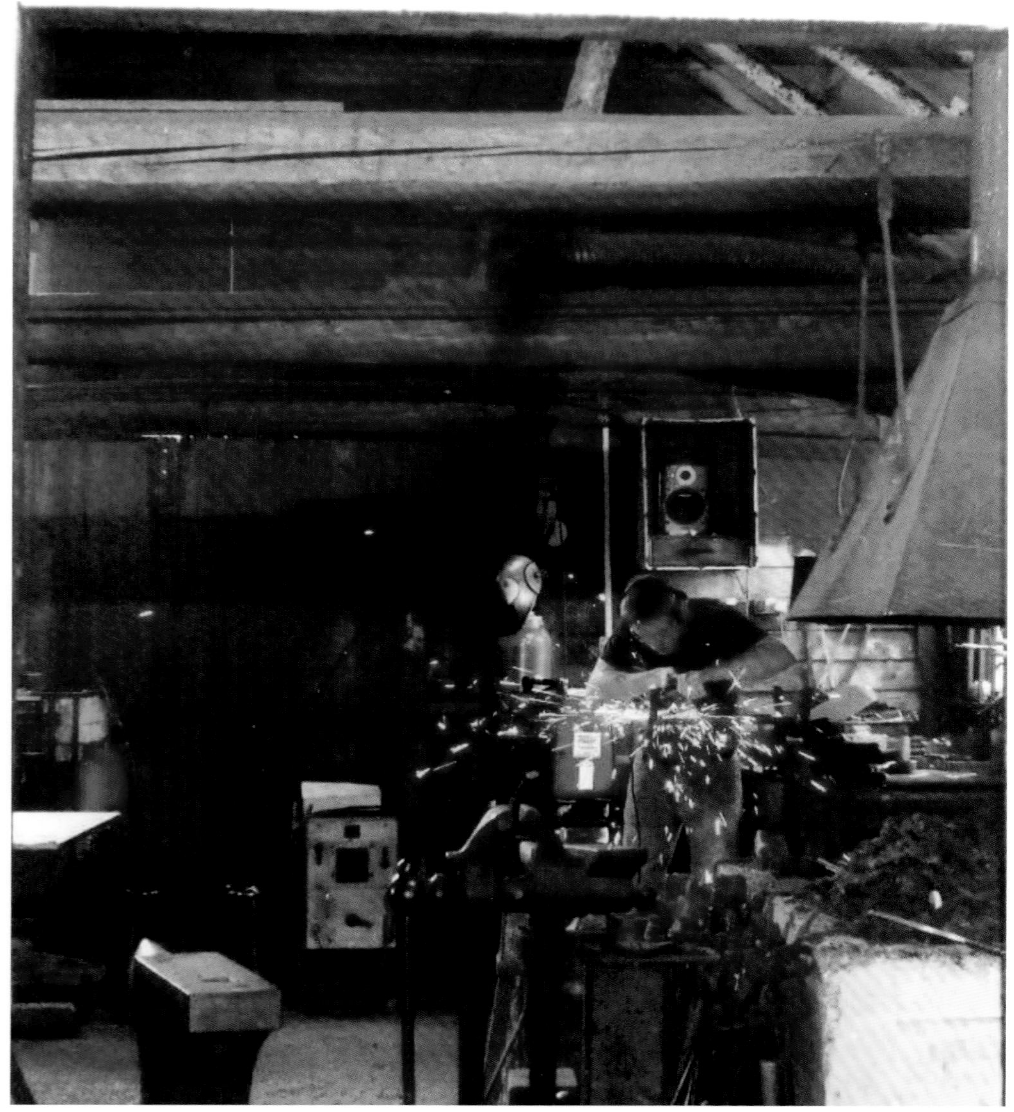

At work in the forge

Charles Normandale's knowledge of engineering, combined with his understanding of the materials with which he works and a sense of artistry, has resulted in the creation of structures both large and small, functional or just amazing to look at, for all sorts of locations: private, public and ecclesiastical.

His creative work has been developed with his business partner, Julie Brooks-Hill, and with the craft being passed on to the next generation, Normandale's business seems to have a long future ahead of it.

Although the works are not open to the public as a tourist attraction, passers-by can often catch a glimpse or sound of work in progress as they go on their way.

An Amazonian woman overlooks the work

Our Lady of Warnford

If you have chosen not to take a diversion via the Monarch's Way to see Charles Normingdale sculptures, your walk will take you South of Warnford, on towards Old Winchester Hill.

However, about a mile north along the A32 is a rather lovely church. It is on a private estate and the entry to the estate might appear somewhat forbidding, with its large, shut gates. The ivy curling around them made me think of something out of a Gothic novel!

Just beside these gates – hidden amongst the ivy – is a small gate, through which you can pass and follow the winding path towards the church of Our Lady of Warnford.

This charming church used to be at the centre of the village. However, when the big house was built, its owners didn't like looking out at the peasants living so close to them, so they moved the village. The work was done by prisoners from the Napoleonic Wars.

I suppose if you are that rich, you may feel that you can do as you like, and such behaviour was not unique to Warnford.

The entry gate

It is rather pleasing that the village (and possibly the peasants) are still there, whereas the house is long gone! Peeping out from the long grass, a crumbling fishily embellished fountain and a few stone steps are all the evidence of what once was.

Canoeists enjoy a Spring day on the River Meon as it winds through the grounds

The flowers that bloom in the Spring, Tra La!

The Mikado; Gilbert and Sullivan

Every year in February, the current owners have an open-day for the locals to enjoy the array of snow-drops in the grounds.

It is an extremely popular event. Cars, nose to tail, edge their way up the driveway towards the carpark on the footprint of the old house. As with so many village events, there is an opportunity to make donations towards the upkeep of the church.

The host, the crowd of gleaming snowdrops is only diminished by the even bigger horde of people, slowly meandering along paths, among woodland, through the remains of the old hall and other long-gone buildings, and beside the river.

Snowdrops flourish on a crisp February day

Beyond the turn in the path is the church, in its quiet location. It fills a gap in local history, fitting neatly between the Saxon Church at Corhampton and the later mediaeval style at Exton (also imitated in the nineteenth century Gothic revival further up the valley at West Meon), in that it is in the Early English style – the beginnings of what we now call Gothic.

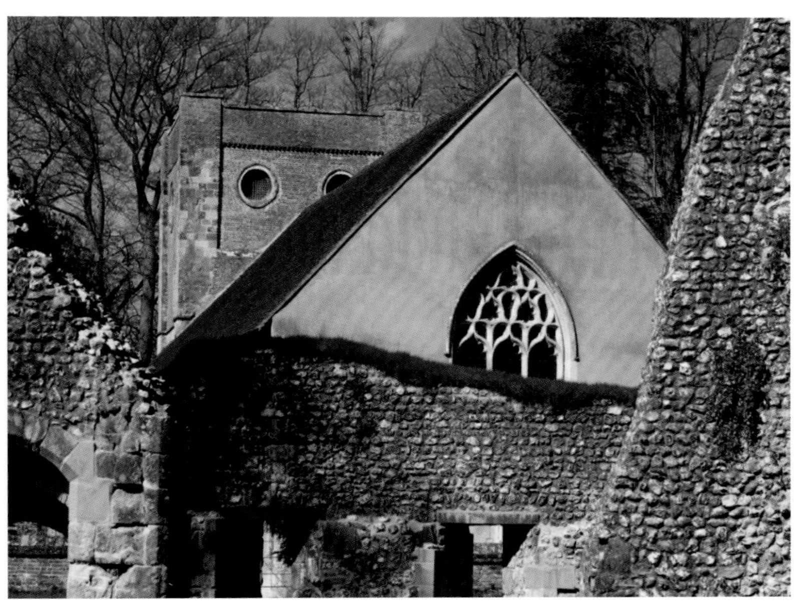

The church, Our Lady of Warnford,
glimpsed through ancient ruins

Earlier ecclesiastical buildings had been on this site at Warnford, established by Saint Wilfred as his base when he attempted to convert the local heathens down at Corhampton and Meonstoke.

The church interior

Inside the present church, it is light and airy, feeling very welcoming (a contrast to those gates). On the East wall, beside the altar, is a very grand tomb to the Neale family. Beautifully restored, it is an excellent example of the Jacobean style, although it is surprising it survived the turmoil of the events leading up to the Commonwealth.

The family's nine children are also represented in a frieze below the effigies of the parents. Four of those tiny figures are holding skulls, indicating that they died before their parents, probably in childhood.

The Neale family tomb, the husband between his two wives and the stunning plinth with their nine children

There is an unusual memorial on the ground to your left, as you make your way down the aisle away from the chancel. The pale stone has carved into it a long thin cross (it could be a crusader's sword) – it marks the resting place of a crusader.

Grave Behaviour

Never on a Sunday? George Lewis's grave

Outside in the churchyard, however, there is another interesting gravestone. Beneath it lie the mortal remains of George Lewis, who met a well-deserved fate (if the carving on the stone shows how the villagers felt about his sacrilegious behaviour).

In the habit of cutting down trees on the Sabbath, one day a bough fell from a tree and crushed him to death! So: he lopped trees and God lopped him!

Considering that Exton's church has the memorial stone to the scholar who spent too much time buried in his books, the local folk obviously believed that the powers from Heaven or Hell would strike down the irreligious!

Therefore, if you are walking on a Sunday, maybe you ought to remember to either clean your boots on Saturday evening or leave the job until Monday morning.

West Meon

Most travellers along the A272 will be familiar with West Meon Hut: once a coaching inn but now much more up-to-date with a petrol station and a family pub. However, few have explored further and found the village of West Meon, just to the South: a delightful place and well worth a visit.

Bath Time!

There are plenty of churches in the area that are built of flint. However, I doubt if there are many of us who would like to find a chunk beneath the bubbles in our baths. The thing is, that is exactly what we do! Well, maybe not 'exactly'. What was once – millions of years ago – a lovely sponge, floating in the Cretaceous seas, over the intervening years has turned into flint. Hard to believe, but true!

The 60,000,000 year-old bath-sponge
HL

In Saxon and Norman times, flint was the building material of choice for churches. The irregular shapes found in the fields were mortared together, generally in neat rows, to form durable walls.

Taking a Knap

By the fourteenth century, tastes were changing: flint knapping (smashing two flints together, creating fissures which would create splitting and the formation of straight edges – sounds simple, doesn't it?) produced regular shapes, often squaring, of the flints. As a result, flushwork – a regular, rather satisfying block pattern of flints – began to be used.

Looking at St John the Evangelist Church in West Meon, you might be lead to believe that you are facing a late mediaeval building illustrating the use of flushwork.

One of a collection of watercolours of the village, this of the village church
(With kind permission of West Meon Primary School)

Great Scott!

However, you are actually looking at an early Victorian building. The Rector was obviously richer than the average vicar of today, as he paid £11,000 towards the cost of £12,000. He was also able to employ the services of the architect George Gilbert Scott, the elder (1811 – 1878). His talents were used for many buildings in that era, especially for churches, but he is perhaps most remembered for edifices like The Royal Albert Memorial in Kensington Gardens and the absolutely stunning St Pancras Station and its adjoining hotel.

I first visited this hotel on one of London's Open House days, when it was still derelict, and was overwhelmed at its beauty and disgusted by its then neglect. Its restoration has received many accolades, and it is certainly worth a visit.

The squared flints used for the building

Although the romantic neo-Gothic style had been popular for some years, it was a pale imitation of late mediaeval Gothic at its best. St John the Evangelist Church was among the first to be influenced by the Cambridge Camden Society's desire to strictly follow the style of the middle ages.

Sir George Gilbert Scott (he was knighted in 1872) is perhaps one of the four best-known British church architects, the others being Sir Christopher Wren, Nicholas Hawksmoor and Augustus Pugin. You may, nevertheless, have favourites of your own to add to this list.

The rare flint work here is stunning: a former vicar, the Reverend Kenneth Wills, described it as 'unique in church building'. These days flint-knappers are hard-to-find highly skilled craftspersons, although an accredited course can be found not too far way in West Sussex at West Dean College. At the time the church in West Meon was built, the flint-knappers were even more local. The village women did the work and were paid one farthing (a quarter of an old penny) for each piece.

Some of the gargoyles. Often modelled on local people or the craftsmen of the church, perhaps some of these were the drunken guests. One, however, looks like queen Victoria, clearly showing the era of the church building.

Raising a glass, or two, or three, or...more...

The altar

In August, 1843, the foundation stone was laid. Such was the importance of the occasion, the Rector wrote to local employers to request they should "give [their] labourers a holiday from three o'clock to enable them to be present in the Church field". Obviously, the workmen felt that this was such a weighty event, it would be impolite not to celebrate enthusiastically. Several men needed a whole week to recover!

When the church was consecrated almost three years later, it was also a day given over to a village holiday. Whether there were any similar consequences, I do not know.

Ashes to Ashes

Over the years, many people have been buried in the churchyard. The parents of William Cobbett – the political reformer, journalist and social commentator, probably best remembered for his book 'Rural Rides' – are reputedly buried here, according to the Reverend Kenneth Wills, although I cannot verify this. Also buried here are the remains of another couple better remembered for their son (but more of that later).

Good Lord!

If you stand on the steps of St John the Evangelist Church, and look back down the pathway, not far off is a flat-topped gravestone. Many of us might be tempted by this horizontal plane to imagine a game of table-tennis played upon its surface. The sport, however, is the wrong one to be associated with the occupant. The gentleman beneath the slab is Thomas Lord, the founder of The Marylebone Cricket Club, more commonly known by its initials. It is 'the custodian and arbiter of' the world of cricket.

Thomas Lord's grave

Thomas Lord portrait (Reproduced by kind permission of MCC)

Thomas Lord was born far away from either Hampshire or London. He hailed from Thirsk in Yorkshire. Born in 1755, he came to London via a childhood in Norfolk. A canny wine merchant, he amassed enough money to support his cricketing interests.

Invited to London by The White Conduit Club, one of his tasks was to find a new venue for them, as their existing ground was in Islington, an area outisde London which was vulnerable to footpads, cut-throats and highwaymen.

With some of the scandals in modern day cricket, perhaps they accidentally took the rogue element with them when they moved from their old ground.

And this match is sponsored by %*?@!#

Thomas Lord was first and foremost a business man, so entry to the new Dorset Fields ground was through his wine shop!

Increasing rents, however, meant another move to a different ground, but the new landlord was less than accommodating regarding the availability of drink. So Thomas Lord happily pocketed £4,000 compensation when the building of the Regent's Canal necessitated yet another move.

They were on to their third site by 1814 but, just over a decade later, Lord was aiming to make more money by selling much of the ground for housing. Well, that was just not cricket! A fellow cricketer (and also a director of the Bank of England) William Ward, bought out Lord's share for £5,000. This site has remained the world renowned cricket ground ever since.

Despite his wheeler-dealing and treachery of trying to sell it off for housing, the ground still bears his name.

Shortly afterwards, he retired to Hampshire, to West Meon, to take up farming. He was bowled out two years later in 1832, and thus is buried in St John the Evangelist's graveyard.

Another of the watercolours owned by the school, of the pub named after Thomas Lord (With kind permission of West Meon Primary School)

The past is another country

The Go-Between; L P Hartley

Today in the village, the most obvious connection to Thomas Lord is the pub named after him. Don't be miss-lead into thinking that, upon his death, the villagers created this monument to their exalted former resident. Until the mid-1950s, this watering hole was called The New Inn and is fondly remembered by Ron Stone who was born there many years ago. Indeed, as the local coalman, his contribution to the community of West Meon has probably been far greater than Mr Lord's!

So, the name of the pub is more marketing ploy than memorial.

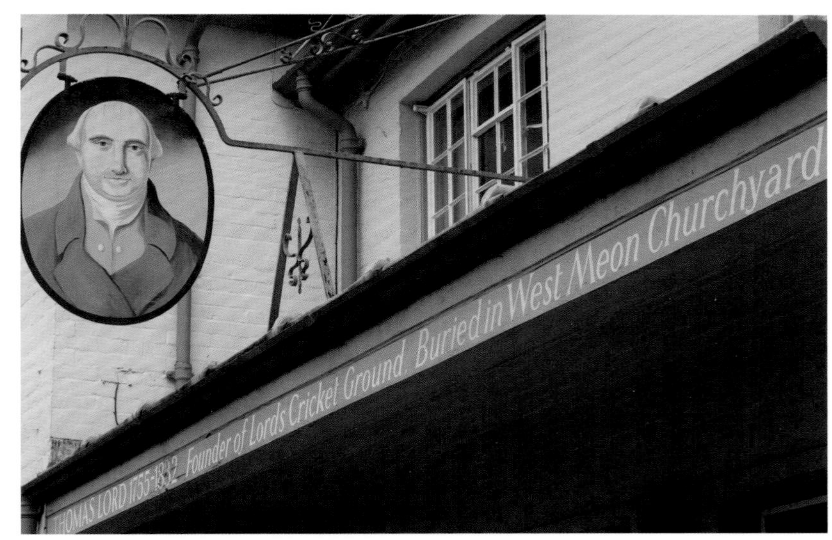

The pub

But times change. In the almost one and a half centuries between the death of Thomas Lord and the renaming of the pub, West Meon went through a period of about sixty years when it would have been unrecognisable to either Lord's contemporaries or to those imbibing at 'his' pub these days. Spanning the village was a huge railway viaduct, as the Meon Valley Railway line steamed its way from North to South. It is difficult to imagine this while strolling around these days, although take a quiet road out of the village to a place reclaimed by nature, and among the long grasses the footings of West Meon Railway Station can still be found.

The well cover in the pub garden: more work by Charles Normandale at Wheely Down

All that remains of the disused station

The old approach road to the station crosses above, on the bridge that spanned the line

Graffiti under the bridge: with the crack in the brickwork looking like a lightning strike, it could be symbolic of the deterioration of the railway.

The Wrong Trousers

A lady in West Meon recalls that, as a child, many years ago, she and her friends would sit on a wall in the village mocking the young gentleman from the big house as he cycled past. He looked so silly in his chosen style of trousers, they would call out his nick-name: "Plus-fours! Plus-fours!"

Stopping his bicycle, he would rebuke the village lasses for their disrespect.

Many years later, she recalled, after his death his ashes were returned to the village to be buried alongside his parents, as he had requested. This was done at night, very secretly, and his interment went unmarked upon the headstone of his father. Many villagers were angry that his wishes had been fulfilled.

This young man in his plus-fours? Guy Burgess, the Russian spy and defector.

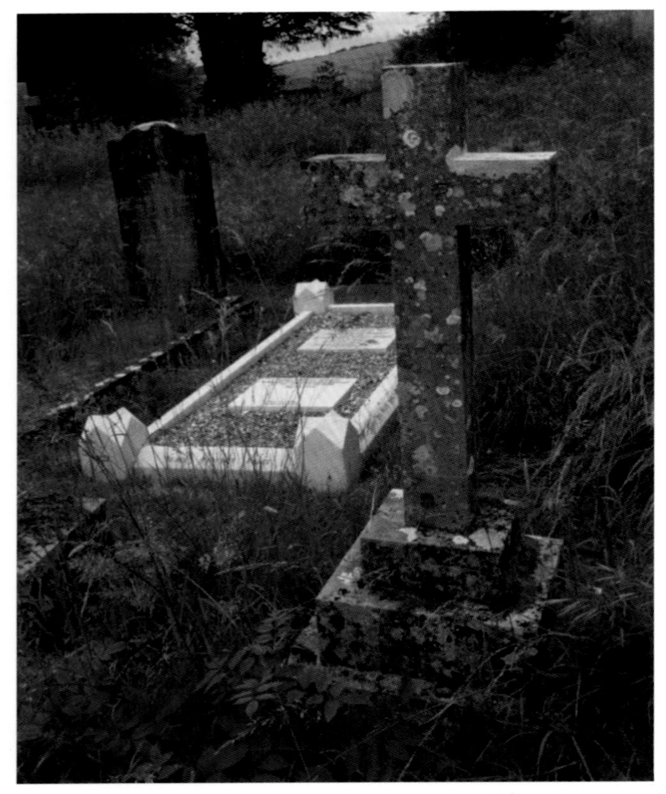

The location of the grave and where the ashes were interred

Eton and Cambridge educated, he was superficially a member of the right-wing Establishment:

> *"Brilliant, flamboyant...he also shot like an arrow to the heart of the Establishment and secretly and systematically betrayed its secrets to the KGB."*
>
> *BBC Radio 4*

He defected to Russia in 1951.

Ironic?

Perhaps it is appropriate that the remains of these two gentlemen are interred in the grounds of a building designed by George Gilbert Scott the Elder, who also designed The Foreign and Commonwealth Office in Whitehall. At the time of its building and for many years afterwards, it was known as the Foreign and Colonial Office. One of these men achieved lasting fame for his promotion of the game of cricket, which was adopted by many countries in our then colonies, who still have an enthusiasm for the game and have world-class teams. The other achieved lasting infamy for behaviour which was anything but 'British'!

Recycling is Nothing New!

When I read about the local women being trained up to knap the flints, I must admit I thought more about the failures than the successes! Although they may have been pretty nifty at shaping the flints as time went by, anyone who has tried a new craft knows all too well that there are many failures to be brushed to one side.

So it was with the flint knapping. There were plenty of disasters. From the beauty of the church, we can see the successes, but what happened to the rejects? Well, they did not go to waste.

As you approached the church, you passed the local primary school. How closely did you look at the stonework of that building? Yes, you've guessed: the unwanted irregular flints from the church were not swept into a pile and buried. They were used in the construction of the village school.

Education is not the filling of a pail, but the lighting of a fire.

W B Yeats (attrib.)

West Meon Primary School was opened in 1852, its cost being £1,393 (eleven and a half per cent of the cost of the church next door). The majority of the money was given by Mary Touchet from Exton. An unusual custom is observed weekly by the children, when fresh flowers are put upon her grave in the neighbouring churchyard.

The school with children playing. All these pictures belong to the school. They were painted and given by a grandfather of one of the pupils some years ago. Now, when the children leave in Year Six, each one is presented with a copy of one of the set of pictures.

(With kind permission of West Meon Primary School)

Not much has changed in the world of education. Victorian reports of extremes of temperature are frequently echoed in modern schools, with their long corridors and doors casually left open!

Absence was ever a problem, but parental notes these days report 'feeling unwell' and various spellings of diarrhoea, whereas in the past seasonal farm labouring took children from their studies, and outbreaks of measles, mumps or scarlet fever could lead to fatalities.

However, the biggest plagues afflicting the school were often outbreaks of head-lice! Plus ça change, plus c'est la même chose.

In days of yore, contagious diseases were a real problem in schools. Nowadays, with immunisation, we rarely get outbreaks of things like mumps or measles. Such was the virulence of these illnesses, and the risk to life so high, that when a member of a household became ill the whole family was barred from school in an attempt to limit the epidemic. Sometimes, for weeks on end, West Meon School would have about half the children absent when such infections were rife.

Mooved to Destruction!

Two somewhat unusual forms of vandalism occurred early last century. One January, a herd of cows broke into the school vegetable garden overnight, eating most of the contents and trampling the rest.

A similar invasion occurred at the start of the Second World War: not the Nazis, but a flock of sheep!

The school's garden (with kind permission of West Meon Primary School)

Perhaps a note on learning is also required here. A decade after the school opened there was concern that, generally, the girls' maths was not as good as that of their male counterparts. However, this was not particularly worrying as – thank goodness – the girls dedicated less time to their sums so that more time could be spent on something that mattered: their needlecraft. Twenty years later, stitching standards had obviously slipped as the infant girls were working without thimbles! The HMI annual report of 1884 stated "...this must never be allowed."

I wonder how future generations will view the average OFSTED report from nowadays.

Rural schools all too frequently are closed as pupil numbers wane and they become unsustainable. In a thriving village like West Meon, perhaps this school will have another 160 years or more!

Chim chim-in-ey, chim chim-in-ey,
Chim chim cher-oo!
There's more to a chimney
than a brush up the flue!

If you continue up the road past the school and the church for about half a mile, you will find the West Meon Pottery.

As a keen potter myself, I entered the premises with curiosity and familiarity. I ground to a halt as I was confronted by an unusually tall kiln. This was not what I had been expecting! This is not a pottery producing day-to-day crocks, jugs for tourists or sculpture for the lounge. The works crafted here are huge. Giant urns for gardens in stately homes sit in the workroom, dwarfed by magnificent chimney pots.

It's easy-peasy to throw a jug or a bowl, but to hand-throw a chimney pot of five feet or more is beyond my imagination. If a house restoration needs a matching pot, then an identical one can be produced here. A modern building, requiring something other than those available at a builders' merchant, could be topped off quite satisfactorily by work made here in West Meon.

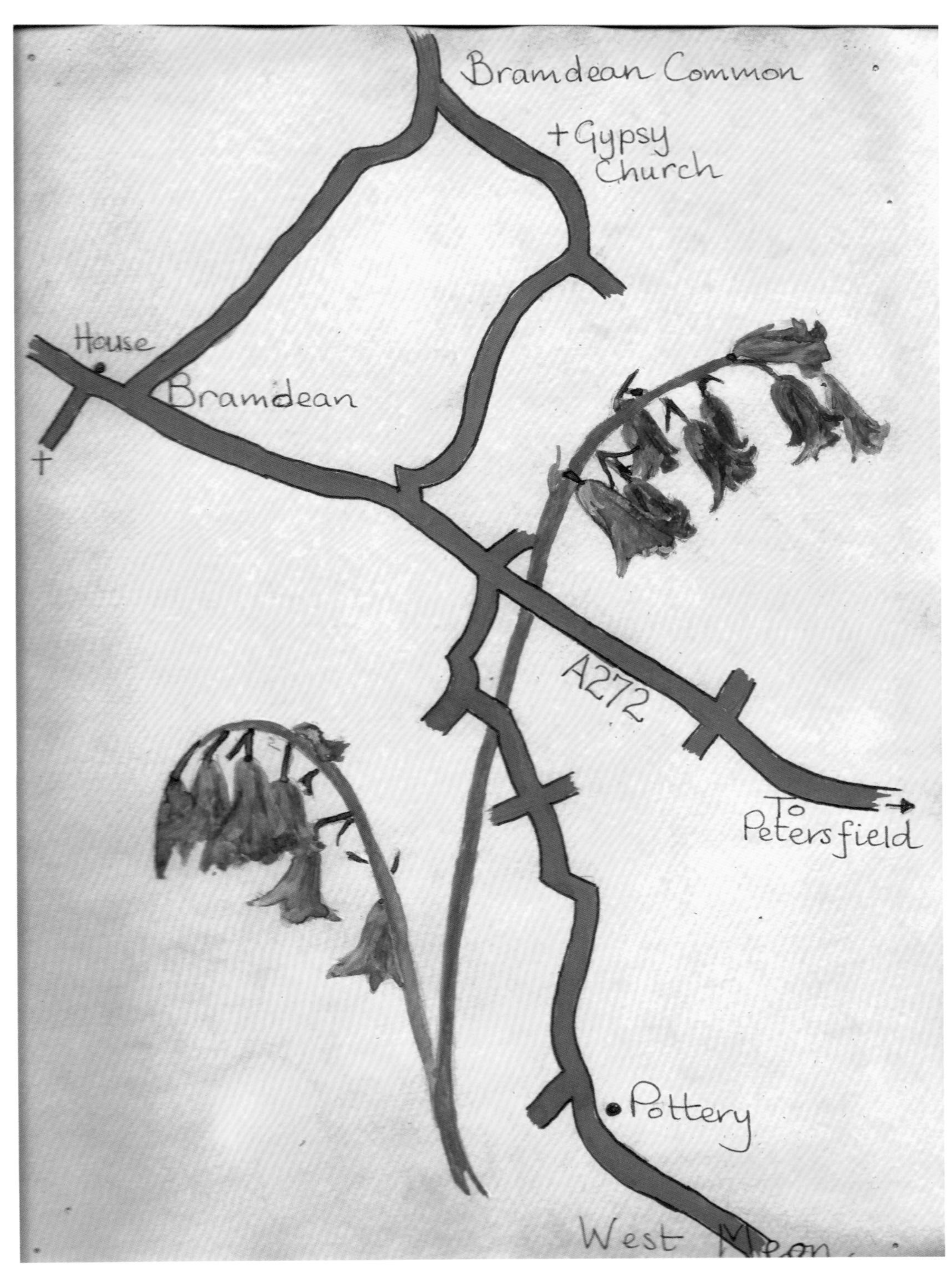
Bramdean Common
+ Gypsy Church
House
Bramdean
+
A272
To Petersfield
Pottery
West Meon

Most of the rich red earthenware clay is local, although other clays from elsewhere in the country are used when required.

As with Charles Normandale's blacksmith's work at Warnford, this is a working site and not generally visited by tourists, although the team will gladly show you their creations if you are particularly interested.

In 1989, nearby Uppark, a National Trust property in West Sussex, was gutted by fire. Restoration took many years and much of the work needed to be newly created, as it was beyond repair. The forty-three new chimney pots were made in this pottery.

Mick Pinner, the owner, standing beside a finished pot, shows how tall one of those tiny chimney-pots on top of a house really is!

Meanwhile the potter demonstrates how they are created

Although I've taken time out to go up and down the Meon Valley, we really ought to be getting back to our route of the South Downs Way. So let's get back to Exton and start walking again.

Across the fields and the A32, the way passes through more farmland before we begin the ascent of Old Winchester Hill.

Old Winchester Hill

Old Winchester Hill is a high point, with wonderful views on a clear day. In ancient times it was an Iron Age fort and the ditches can be seen today. Now it's one of Hampshire's National Nature Reserves, so an ideal place to pause and take in the surroundings.

The Iron-age hill fort

There are information boards around the area to let you know its history and also what to look out for, so for picnickers this is a lovely lunch-spot on a sunny day!

Rolling Stones

There is a legend that, when the Romans came to our shores, the site was decided upon for the building of a major centre, hence the name 'Old Winchester'. Its high location would indeed have made it a defensive success. On the other hand, it's a long way uphill for the water supplies to be lugged! The legend is that, during the daytime, the Roman's workforce would man-handle large pieces of stone to the top ready for the building work. Nevertheless, by morning the stones had – as if by magic – rolled back down to the bottom. After many attempts, they gave up and chose the location we know as Winchester today.

Now, there are some legends that I'm willing to look at seriously, but this one is rather too extreme. After all, if the Romans had really settled upon this hill-top, they would not have left the stones so precariously balanced that a puff of wind would have toppled them all the way back down to Warnford. These are the guys that introduced sanitation, medicine, education, wine, public order, irrigation, roads and of course, not forgetting the viaduct, to England, so I'm certain that they had the civil engineering skills to keep the stones at the top. Perhaps, had they really tried to use the hill-top for their city, the building materials were rather too tempting to leave *lying around for any locals intent upon some DIY.*

Butterflies and harebells showing the typical wildlife you will find in this spot

Also, if it had been abandoned by the Romans who'd been planning their city, surely it would be called Antiquus Venta Belgarum Collis, not Old Winchester Hill!

I Know a Bank Where the Wild Thyme Blows

A Midsummer Night's Dream; Wm. Shakespeare

In season, chalk hill blue and meadow brown are among the dozens of different species of butterflies that can be seen here, as well as many mammals and birds.

Twitchers would be well advised to bring their binoculars! From buzzards and blackcaps to wheatears and willow warblers, the dipping and diving can give pleasure to anyone, but especially to those 'in the know' about birdlife.

Grasses and flowers enhance the landscape throughout the year, but especially in early summer when so many varieties are in bloom, attracting the pollinating insects. To help maintain the landscape, grazing sheep keep things under control. The hilliness of the area means that the breeds need to be selected carefully. So, once again, it could be a Herdwick looking at you sheepishly!

It seems that this breed – a cross between a sheep and a teddy bear – could have been introduced into this country from Norway, brought over by the Vikings! Genetically, they have been found to have a match with their ovine Scandinavian cousins.

From the old fort, the site of the Meon Valley railway line – long closed down – can be seen. Known as The Strawberry Line, in times gone by the abundant harvest of fruit would be transported to the London markets by train, taking summer delights to those in the industrialised heartlands, and bringing financial reward to the countryside.

Herdwicks also graze here at Winchester Hill

People enjoying time out at Winchester Hill

Progressus Iter

The South Downs Way leads North from the prehistoric site. After crossing the road and seeming to backtrack to the West for a few hundred metres, the path heads downward towards a very pleasant valley with farm buildings at the bottom.

On the day that I went there the rain bucketed down, and with my waterproofs on and my hood tied closely around my head, I went straight past Meon Springs, missing a really delightful location! Ah well: such is life!

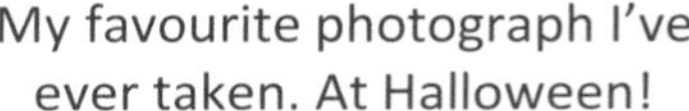

My favourite photograph I've ever taken. At Halloween!

Camping and Glamping

On a return visit, I discovered what I had missed. For a start, there are refreshments! From a morning bacon roll to baguettes with coffee, this can mean that you don't have to carry so much in your rucksack. On the other hand, when they have events, you might find yourself limited to the confectionery! As this is a business and not a provision for walkers, it is an added bonus, not an expectation!

If you've booked in advance, then there is accommodation. It's one of the few places where you don't have to step off your route to get a night's sleep. With your own tent, things are relatively easy, but if you have arranged it in advance, then you can step into the luxury of a yurt!

Some of the variety of accommodation you'll find along the South Downs Way

Catch your Tea!

For those enjoying a more leisurely break, you could make even greater use of the facilities here. Bring your own rod and tackle and (I'm imagining here that you came by car, not that you've got the stuff in your rucksack) there is the chance to relax with some fishing.

You won't be in Wordsworthian isolation: I was surprised when I visited how many day-trippers lined the banks. Some people had travelled quite a distance because they enjoy the location – I chatted with a father and son from Reading who frequently enjoy

days-out here, as well as with a soldier who likes a spot of fishing when he's on leave.

If you are without all the bits and bobs and without knowledge and skill, then you can even book a lesson!

With the lakes and their banks, the variety of trees and the beautiful landscape, it is certainly worth pausing here...unless, of course, the rain is tipping down!

On reflection, let's have fish for tea tonight!

Let's take stock!

Yes, Meon Springs is a delightful location to fish and relax. But let's not forget that the Fishery is also a workplace. In fact, every mile of the South Downs Way is someone's place of employment in one way or another, be it in the leisure or service industries, trade or in production, especially the production of our food: veggies, meat or dairy.

Whitewool – Meon Springs – is also a working livestock farm. The team there happily welcomes pre-arranged groups of visitors to the farm, and this can be an eye-opening experience for some of us townies who only shop at the local supermarket, and don't always appreciate where the food in our trolleys comes from.

Indeed, on occasions, I have explained to teenagers on walks the difference between cows and bulls: cows have what looks like a rubber glove dangling between their legs, and ramblers are like red rags to a bull. Which is, of course, nonsense as cattle are colour-blind and it is the flapping about, not the colour, which makes a bull go wild!

And just because you've worked out that it's a field of cows, don't think that they're placid. A rambling friend was corralled by a herd of cows. Having escaped to a nearby pub, the landlord told him this was not uncommon and they often got desperate phone-calls from penned in walkers. Surely a mooving experience!

Cows are bigger and more solid than most of us think, and quickly drive away any memories of Ermintrude or the panto's Buttercup! My shaken friend advises treating them with respect...and think of the accompaniment to the horse-radish with your next pub meal!

Moove along then, dear.
This is my patch!

Curious cows can get dangerously frisky if you've got a dog with you, so don't forget that your pooch is more nimble than you'd think and is most likely to escape. So, drop the lead and edge away as the cows show interest in your dog and you are both more likely to survive.

But once off the lead, do we really know what our family pet is getting up to beyond that ridge in the field? Most of the time the dog has just lost a race with a rabbit or barked ferociously at a butterfly.

Mum with her lambs

However, occasionally they've played a lively barking game with some sheep, and a stressed ewe will lose the lambs that she is carrying.

The term "sheep-worrying" is a misnomer – they are not simply puzzled about two-legged creatures shouting "Mint sauce!" at them.

Among those working at Whitewool Farm is Terena Plowright, who maintains her own animals, including sheep. Terena is an enthusiastic ambassador for farming, including organising her own shows and encouraging visitors to learn about animal husbandry and life in the countryside.

Such is Terena's concern about the welfare of livestock, she aims to educate dog lovers about the ghastly consequence a moment's lack of forethought can bring about. Gathering information nationally through her Facebook page has highlighted the enormity of the problem and hopefully raised the issue in the consciousness of all of us who love visiting the countryside.

It's worth remembering that in every dog there potentially lurks a big bad wolf, and as we get that feeling of freedom from being in the open air, so do our dogs. And their bite can be worse than their bark. One dog not on a lead can leave behind a scene of carnage – severely injured animals or, all too frequently, dead sheep. Just ask Terena!

A charity walk along the South Downs Way

I wanna be a hero!

The basic rule is: you can walk through the field, making sure you reclose the gate, and if you leave the animals alone, they will leave you alone.

Today, however, while walking in Kent, I came across the exception that proves the rule. My companion noticed a ewe on her back, too exhausted to even wave her legs much, with her two lambs hungry and distressed. One of them was even trying to suckle her prone mum. Weighed down with wool at this time of year, she would probably have died. We scaled the padlocked gate (hinge end) and gently rolled her onto her side. She sprang to her feet and the little ones immediately plugged themselves in for a draught lunch. We returned to our walk, feeling rather pleased with ourselves, despite there being not even a bleat of thanks!

A view to the West. Look back as you progress, and you can just see Winchester, your starting point, in the morning haze.

East Meon

Although the route takes a sharp right turn at Halnaker Lane, if you choose to go straight on, you will arrive at East Meon.

It is another attractive village, although it has an extra feature: you will find the budding River Meon running through the village by the side of the main road, traversing the houses.

The source of this river is a spring, just a few hundred yards South of the village. However, despite following a meandering path through a farm, the overgrowth was so thick, I found it was impossible to reach!

It's a brave soul who ventures any further towards the Meon's source!

Whereas some villages along the way can lay claim to both noteworthy and notorious figures, East Meon seems to be a little short of either heroes or villains. King John, before he inherited his brother Richard's crown, frequented the area, but otherwise, despite a pub named The Izaak Walton (this famous gentleman fished in the area and spent his final few years nearby), East Meon is rather low down on the list of ownership of the famous or infamous.

Oh dear: with the pairs of antonyms in the paragraph above, I'm rather worried I've caught a dose of Jane Austenism from spending too many days in her home county!

Nevertheless, with a church, a school, two pubs and a village shop, this village in comparatively well blessed with amenities and can provide the walker with a leisurely lunch or an overnight stop.

These days with country pubs falling by the wayside, it's good to find a village with two watering-holes!

It is worth remembering that, although the South Downs Way does not have as many 'followers' as the more iconic long-distance paths (for example the Coast-to-Coast up North), we (the walkers) do make a contribution to the local economy. The survival of shops and pubs is helped by our passing trade. In turn, this survival helps to maintain the villages which make the area such a pleasant place to walk.

*Now, back to the village itself. East Meon has a thriving history society. Their website is extremely thorough and has a wealth of interesting information. It is certainly worth a read before visiting the area (*www.eastmeonhistory.net*). Also, the village shop has a guide book for sale so you can have a self-guided tour.*

No longer do villages have the butcher, the baker and the candlestick maker, as in days of yore, so it is good to see how many do have at least one shop

It is one of the largest parishes in the area, with a population of well over a thousand people. In the Domesday Book of 1086 it is recorded that there were six mills in the area and enough land for sixty four ploughs. Nine hundred years later, the Hampshire Museums Service, in conjunction with the Sunday Times, chose this village to represent the 'Domesday Village'. A model was constructed of how the village probably looked and, following its display in Winchester, it was taken to the museum at Bayeux where, I believe, it is still displayed.

The community spirit can be seen in village life, for example the weekly quiz night at the Izaak Walton. Don't think that it is restricted to the locals: they will make visitors welcome, although it is probably not a good thing to turn up in a group and win, as I did on my first visit!

However, they did not bear a grudge, and I was warmly welcomed on my next visit, when I was invited to join in with a team of the regulars!

Among the highlights are the church and the fourteenth century courthouse.

The Doomsday village: created by the people of East Meon at the Millennium to show how the village would have looked in 1066 and now on display in France

Although the courthouse is now a private house, it can be seen from the churchyard. It was commissioned by William Wykeham – the founder of Winchester College – as his seat of power as Bishop meant he was also lord of the manor.

Here's the church, and here's the steeple
Open the door and see all the people

traditional

All Saints' Church has several interesting features, which makes it worth a visit as it has 'something-for-everyone', as well as its spiritual purpose. For those with an enthusiasm for ecclesiastical architecture and furniture, it has a great deal of great merit and for those whose fancy is tickled by the arts, there is a tapestry to admire. And for people who like the unusual, there is a carved stone in the wall!

All Saints' Church was described by Nikolaus Pevsner, the scholar and commentator on historical architecture, as 'one of the most thrilling in Hampshire'.

It is largely Norman in construction – easily identifiable by the tops of the window arches, which are semi-circular. There are other parts where the windows are larger and rather pointy. This Early English style is indicative of the additions during the reign of King Henry III (the son of King John).

All Saints' mediaeval font

Inside the church, near to the door, is a rare font – a gift to the church from the Bishop of Winchester, Henry of Blois – the one interred in the Cathedral. The font is in black marble from Tournai (now part of Belgium). Its four sides are carved, two of them showing the story of Adam and Eve.

Henry of Blois was the brother of King Stephen, and a major player on the

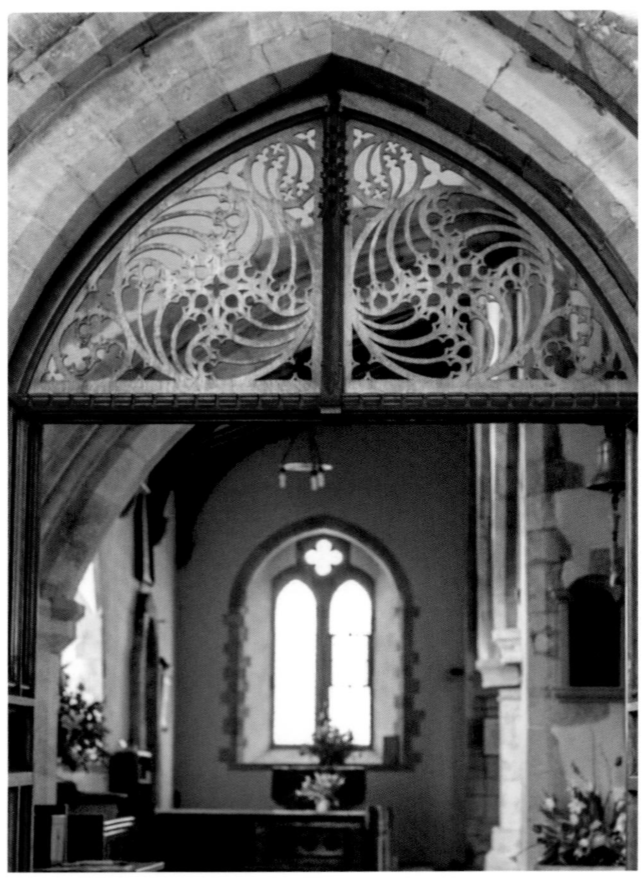
The beautiful craftsmanship from down the centuries helps to make the church feel very welcoming

political scene of the era, during the Civil War between Stephen and his cousin the Empress Matilda. However, he was rather self-serving and would change sides at the drop of a mitre.

In a period when people believed their actions in this world could jeopardize their chances of Saint Peter allowing access through the Pearly Gates, Henry of Blois obviously needed to compensate for his less than charming behaviour, so donating a gift like the font to East Meon was worth a few extra points on the score sheet.

Internally, much of the other beautiful design is influenced by the Arts and Crafts movement, when Sir Ninian Cooper was employed in the early twentieth century. The altar and the timber screens are his work. He also designed the World War One memorial East window.

On the eastern wall of the nave there is a small stone engraved with the words 'Amens Plenty'. Originally, this was on the floor nearby. When lifted, it was found to mark where four Civil War combatants had been buried upright! Upright burials are not unique, but with four of them in there, it must have been rather cosy.

Bringing us up to the current century, there is a beautiful tapestry on display. It was created by a team of local embroiderers to celebrate the Millennium in 2000, although it took several years to complete.

Like the Domesday Book from almost 1000 years earlier, the tapestry documents the properties and people within the village. Although not strictly ecclesiastical, the church seems the right place for it to be displayed, as it is spiritually the centre of the community.

The vivid green border is redolent of the tapestry, from half a century earlier, in Coventry Cathedral of Christ in Majesty, behind the altar there.

Money buys lands, and wives are sold by fate

<u>The Merry Wives of Windsor</u>: Wm. Shakespeare

Although earlier I dismissed East Meon for lacking famous people, there is, however, one John Lackland, otherwise known as John, Earl of Mortain and also as King John!

More than once I was told by locals that King John had been married in East Meon. This is difficult to verify, as there is a great deal of evidence to the contrary. "All good myths start with a germ somewhere" they say, so perhaps it is worth considering this myth.

John married twice. Confusingly, both wives were called Isabelle. The second bride, Isabelle of Angouleme, was married to him in the year 1200 at Bordeaux. We would raise an eyebrow about this marriage today as – although we cannot be absolutely sure – it is probable she was aged about twelve! And the marriage was fruitful, with five children!

But let's get back to bride number one, Isabelle of Gloucester. There is clear evidence that the marriage took place between John and his first wife at Marlborough Castle in

Wiltshire in August 1189.

A gateway through to the mediaeval courthouse

However, the marriage was agreed between their fathers when the children were much younger (she was about four and he eight). As King Henry II, John's father, was such a cunning fox and had established the importance of the law following the chaos of King Stephen's reign, I can't see him not making sure there were no legal loopholes in the contract. Also, there seems to have been some sort of marriage agreement two years later, in 1176. Having agreed a contract between the pair, it is quite likely that a betrothal would have taken place, and in mediaeval times it would have been as binding as a marriage.

Isabelle's father, the Earl of Gloucester (the son of Robert, the illegitimate son of King Henry I and half-brother of Matilda – John's grandmother), had ownership of the land around East Meon. Therefore, upon their marriage in 1189, the title of the land would have become Prince John's. As the land is in the See of Winchester, it would have been an ideal location for the betrothal.

Perhaps – and this is entirely speculation on my part – it may have been that the betrothal took place in All Saints' Church, East Meon, where her father had land.

After all the fall-out from a little trouble in Canterbury Cathedral on Christmas Day, 1170, King Henry II was trying to placate the Church in his dealings. Becket's replacement, Richard of Dover, was on Henry's business during 1176, escorting the King's daughter Joan to her own marriage with the King of Sicily. The second most eminent churchman in England – to all practical purposes – was the Bishop of Winchester, Henry's statesman Richard of Ilchester. It would have made sense to have had any Church blessing of the betrothal conducted by an ally of the King, within the See of Winchester, on land owned by Prince John.

It would also have been useful to involve the Church in these dealings, as Isabelle of Gloucester and Prince John were related: her grandfather was the half-brother to his grandmother. The laws of consanguinity were quite strict and this betrothal was considered rather dodgy!

However, in Henry's view this was a marriage opportunity not to be missed. At the time, John had four older surviving brothers, so it was less important that it should be a political alliance and more likely it was a bond for land and money, both of which were useful for a royal dynasty that was constantly at war with its neighbours. And Isabelle's father was rich! So much so, Henry passed a law disinheriting her sisters so that Isabelle would get everything.

I ought to state that the National Archive in London does have a reference to some sort of betrothal agreement between the couple in the mid-1180s, but as the bride's father was already dead, it seems too late for a binding agreement between the parents.

Shortly after the betrothal in 1176, Prince John's new 'wife' inherited huge estates upon the death of her father, making John the second largest land-owner in the country after the King...which makes his nickname of Lackland seem rather baffling.

So, the legend of King John actually marrying in East Meon has to remain a legend because there is documentation showing that both of his marriages happened elsewhere. But the story, handed down through the generations, may have a germ of truth, as it is plausible that a contract for a future marriage may have been confirmed in the parish! I'd hate to destroy a local legend, but this is the best I can do to make sense of the story!

Eventually, John and Isabelle of Gloucester married in Marlborough, a few weeks after Henry II died. However, the Pope declared, as they were half-second-cousins (twice removed), 'intimate relations' were forbidden. Bad enough for any young man, but once he unexpectedly became the King in 1199 and needed an heir, it was an absolute disaster!

Of course this raises another possibility. After all, it is a truth universally acknowledged that a (young) man in possession of all his faculties must be in want of a 'wife', and if his real wife was unavailable, John may well have had his 'bit on the side'. If the chosen lady was from the East Meon area, the local rumour-mill could have produced sack-loads of stories, including one about marriage.

One of the many pretty cottages in the village

Ring a ring of roses...

anon

East Meon has always been a large parish, extending at one time as far as the outskirts of Petersfield. For that reason, when the need arose to place a pest house – to contain the victims of disease in the days before immunisation and infection control – within the parish (but as far away from the villagers as possible), it was built near Stroud, North-West of the village, by what is now the A272.

I recall being taught at school about the Great Plague sweeping through London in 1665. Mortalities are estimated to have been around 100,000: about 15% of the population. Then came the Great Fire which destroyed property and livelihoods but allegedly cleansed the city of the pestilence.

The mortality records for this period showed a weekly decline in the number of victims of the plague by this time anyway, so the effects of the fire may have been coincidental.

What we often forget is that it was a national disaster and, although the number of victims was dropping in 1666, there was no helpful fire for the rest of the population of England. A further 30,000 deaths were recorded nationally for that period.

The plague had come and gone like the ebb and flow of the tide over many years. For example, William Shakespeare's son Hamnet died in 1596 at a time when there was an outbreak in Stratford-upon-Avon in Warwickshire.

It was not until 1603 that the law required the collation of Bills of Mortality, which gave a more accurate figure. Between 1603 and 1665 there were only four years when there were no reported plague deaths throughout the country. Surprisingly, 1665 did not have the highest totals when the whole of England is viewed. That was 1625, and a year in which East Meon was particularly affected.

In 1666, Petersfield is recorded as having 235 victims. Despite shutting up infected households to prevent contagion, surrounding areas – including East Meon – were at

risk. The last recorded case in England was in 1679 and plague was removed from the list of categories on the Bills of Mortality in 1703, the year East Meon opened its own Pest House, with room for four families.

Let's not forget: there were other diseases that caused equal fear, for example smallpox, with a thirty percent mortality rate.

Illnesses for which these days treatments are available, in those days caused great fear, so to be able to quarantine victims was progress. Despite being too late to benefit those afflicted by plague in the seventeenth century, East Meon was ahead of the times with its 1703 Pest House: it was not until 1720 that a paper 'A Short Discourse Concerning Pestilential Contagion' was published. This recommended the adoption of the pest house system nationally at public expense, and that the common practice of shutting up families in their own homes, condemning the inhabitants to death, should be discontinued.

Surviving records show what, in those days, would have been the considerable expense of caring for people struck down by an outbreak of smallpox:

> "1727 Dec 16 What we have paid for the people with the small pox 10s. 9d." By February 3 such weekly payments had risen to a peak of £2 1s. 4¾d., thereafter tailing off until mid-March when that particular outbreak had subsided.

Local History Magazine 53: January/February 1996

Please Sir...

<u>Oliver Twist</u>; Charles Dickens

Many of these pest houses operated until 1834 when the new Poor Laws introduced the greatly feared workhouses, stigmatising inmates and meting out atrocious care. Previous poor laws had set up similar systems. East Meon Pest House was superseded by Petersfield Workhouse, ironically in Love Lane.

The Pest House still exists, well away from the village. Whereas the four isolation rooms each had its own entrance, and the upstairs rooms had outside staircases, with the thatched roof now replaced by tiles and those stairways long gone, this hidden away little gem could be mistaken now for just any home. If it was not for the small inscription on the front, no-one would know this pleasant little cottage has such an interesting past.

This is the way the gentlemen ride

nursery rhyme

The early part of the nineteenth century had seen hard times throughout rural Britain, and East Meon was no exception to the destitution affecting many. This was recorded by William Cobbett (he whose parents may have been interred in West Meon churchyard). A diarist and social reformer, he traversed the countryside of South East England and the Midlands on horseback, describing the landscape and its people, commenting upon the agricultural depression and the hardship of the population. His observations were published in 1830, in a book called 'Rural Rides'.

It's not hard to find where in Farnham William Cobbett was born!

Particularly, he strove for reform of the Parliamentary system, which was rife with corruption. Equally, he fought for agricultural reform, principally of the Corn Laws, which had resulted in impoverishment for many farm workers, and also a surge of human fodder for the new factories in the growing cities of the Industrial Revolution.

He supported the cause of agricultural workers, like those at Owslebury who had participated in the Swing Riots. They were protesting against these changes, which discriminated against the farm labourers and small farmers. Indeed, although the riots took place throughout southern England, Hampshire had more disturbances than any other county.

Cobbett is also buried in the town where he was born

Following the defeat of Napoleon in 1815, trade had resumed between Britain and France. Imported cheap grain resulted in the price a farmer could charge for his produce dropping by fifty percent. The House of Commons – representing landowners – legislated, introducing taxes which severely restricted imports.

The new laws protected the profits of the landowners but did nothing to help the poor. Inflated grain prices meant that people could not afford bread, a major part of everyday meals. There were food riots all over Britain.

William Cobbett's writing laid bare the devastation in Hampshire, among other places, and he helped to secure the abolition of the hated Corn Laws.

As he travelled around, he was particularly impressed with the scenic landscape he saw as he rode towards East Meon:

"I should have dwelt long upon the beauties of the place."

Rural Rides; 24th November, 1822

Lifting up mine eyes unto the hills – or tower – at All Saints'

In particular, he commented on the age and splendour of the village's church, citing its stunning Norman tower.

However, its size – he noted – seemed exceptionally large for the local population. The reason, he deduced, was that so many of the farms had been neglected as the workers had left for the city in expectation of jobs:

...the many square miles of downs near this village (East Meon), all bearing the marks of the plough, and all out of tillage for many years... It is the destructive murderous paper system that has transferred the fruit of the labour and the people along with it...to the neighbourhood of the all-devouring Wen*.

Rural Rides; 24th November, 1822

Travel south-west to Botley near Southampton to find where William Cobbett lived for several years

---

** It is worth noting that 'Wen' has two meanings. Firstly, it is the sprawling city. Secondly, it is a blemish or cyst on the skin, making Cobbett's chosen word an interesting metaphor.*

Prior to this, East Meon had, over many years, taken care of its own in times of hardship:

> ...the parish was still a family as regards the care of the poor. A family is bound to shelter its weaker members, so it was thought right for the parish...to be responsible for the impotent and destitute within its borders.
>
> Hampshire Review, Autumn 1950;
> 'An Old-time Workhouse' by Reverend G Lacey-May

From 1727, East Meon had had its own workhouse, in response to an Act of Parliament five years earlier, which attempted to reduce the cost to parishes of providing 'parochial relief'. By removing the needy to the provided workhouse, those who chose not to enter were no longer regarded as the responsibility of the parish.

These early workhouses were not as horrific as the picture painted by Charles Dickens in 'Oliver Twist', describing how, by the following century, they had become oppressive, shameful institutions.

> Oliver cried lustily. If he could have known that he was an orphan, left to the tender mercies of churchwardens and overseers, perhaps he would have cried the louder.
>
> (Chapter One)

In East Meon, the inmates grew their own vegetables, bred pigs, baked their own bread and did the repairs and maintenance of the building. So, although some cost was involved, it was – to a degree – self-supporting. Considering the hardships caused by the Corn Laws, the inmates had a measure of welfare better than some of their fellow villagers:

Ironically, inmates may have been better housed, fed, clothed and generally more comfortable than many a villager dwelling elsewhere.

Hampshire Review, Autumn 1950;
'An Old-time Workhouse' by Reverend G Lacey-May

This workhouse building, redundant after the establishment of the one in Petersfield, burnt down in 1910, although those exploring the village today can see the lane marked on the map in which it once stood.

And here is an interesting little extra about William Cobbett. In 1802 he began publishing debates from the House of Commons. His printer was a man called Thomas Hansard. So, when Cobbett was having a few financial troubles in 1812, he passed this over to his printer. Thus it is that we refer to Hansard today to check on events in Parliament and don't call for a copy of Cobbett!

The High Street memorial in Botley

William Cobbett bought a small farm in Botley, on the outskirts of Southampton and settled down from 1805 until 1817. One hundred and fifty years later, a commemorative stone was erected in the town centre.

Nature adds drama, looking Eastwards from the village towards the Downs at Butser Hill

The curfew tolls the knell of parting day

Elegy Written in a Country Churchyard; Thomas Gray

Should you choose to stay on the route of the South Downs Way, rather than go to the village of East Meon, then you will have turned right at Halnaker Lane. A broad woodland path continues to run in a southerly direction along an open escarpment. Upon reaching the road, the route takes a left hand turn right, past the Sustainability Centre.

Looking back over the previous pages, a great deal of information focuses on the churches. This is not surprising. After all, many of these buildings have endured over the centuries, reflecting political and social change as well as architectural styles and artistic taste.

Most importantly for the traveller, they are – despite theft and vandalism – generally open to the public and offering sanctuary from the elements (not from the law, as in earlier times), which can make them excellent places to pause.

As the churches are generally in the middle of communities, they can reflect the customs and the people who lived there. For centuries, when those people died, their mortal remains were buried in the church grave-yard and frequently marked either with a headstone or with a memorial within the church itself.

There at the foot of yonder nodding beech

Elegy Written in a Country Churchyard; Thomas Gray

In more recent times, many interments have taken place in larger cemeteries or the remains have been cremated. With the latter, there may be a small marker in the churchyard, or often they are noted in the book of remembrance at the crematorium. The ashes can often be taken to a place that had particular significance for the departed.

In the last few years a new way has been adopted by some families: a natural, sustainable burial. Here, at the Sustainability Centre, within the South Downs National Park, is a woodland area, overlooking pasture and with views towards the coast, where interments can take place in a natural, dignified way.

Graves are not marked with headstones, but with wild flowers, and a register is kept, as well as a plan to help families find the resting place of their loved ones. It is a beautiful and peaceful location.

I love to go a-wandering,
Along the mountain track,
and as I go, I love to sing,
My knapsack on my back.

adapted from: Florenz Friedrich Sigismund (1788-1857)

For some, therefore, this area has become a final resting place. For others, it can be a one-night resting place (either in a tent or with a proper roof over their heads) or just a place to pause for a cuppa and a snack.

Cyclists on the South Downs Way having a break at the café at the Sustainability Centre

For the more determined walkers from Winchester, this can make a much needed first overnight stop. Those taking a more leisurely approach, like me, may find it is the right place for the second night.

Wetherdown Lodge from the paddock

Some of the buildings look rather dilapidated but, as money becomes available, these 1960s ex-Ministry of Defence buildings are being repaired and renovated.

You may find this location marked as HMS Mercury on your map. Yes: the buildings are sited on a piece of land that was really a ship! Really! The Royal Navy has a habit of naming its land bases just like it does its sea-craft. Thus the area was for many years a Royal Navy listening station called HMS Mercury.

Previously, the land had another life as a big house with an estate. During the twentieth century, the area has had three uses: a big house (these days divided into privately owned apartments); a Royal Navy base; and a centre for the environmentally aware!

Family-time in a short break in a yurt

It's the rich what gets the pleasure...

anon

A Tamworth Pig at Staunton Country Park

The family who lived in the big house, Leydene House, was the Peels – descendants of Robert Peel, a textile merchant's son who created the Metropolitan Police, introduced the Factory Act to Parliament and reintroduced income-tax (not the most popular thing to do). As well as all this, he bred the first Tamworth pigs (known by the people of Tamworth as Sandybacks) by crossing a local breed with pigs from Ireland. Oh, and he was Prime Minister from 1834 until 1835, and again from 1841 to 1846.

Police officers have been given a variety of nicknames over the years, some affectionate and some rather less so. 'Peelers' and 'bobbies' are names stemming directly from the name of Robert Peel. However, some sources suggest that the abusive term 'pigs' could have a less offensive derivation: after all, Sir Robert Peel did create a breed of pig as well as creating the police force! I'd like to think this is so!

I can't think of any Prime Minister in modern times who has usefully had their fingers in so many pies!

Now, the Lord Peel (William Robert Wellesley Peel) who lived at Leydene House was the grandson of this famous Prime Minister. He too was a politician, but did not rise to the same dizzy heights as his

But this porker is a Hampshire Black: a local breed!

grandfather. Curiously, though, he was the one granted a more illustrious title, being made an Earl in 1929.

Like her husband, Lady Peel had antecedents in the textile industry. Her grandfather, James Williamson (later Lord Ashton), invented linoleum. So proud was she of her family's creation, Lady Eleanor Peel used the patterns decorating the flooring material as the template for the design of her flowerbeds at Leydene! Somewhere in this, I ought to say, the couple had one son, who became the Earl of Clanfield.

So, let's be honest: she was not short of a bob or two! Upon her marriage into the Peel family, her father gave her a rather nice wedding gift. No, not a toaster, but £800,000. That's over £588 million in today's value. So, their marriage could be considered a marriage of convenience: his title and status for her money. This was topped up in 1930 when her father died. She got a further five million pounds. That's the equivalent of another £1,427 million in this day and age.

Leydene House was not an ancient edifice to an antediluvian aristocratic family. It was incredibly new. Lord and Lady Peel spent some time in 1913 looking for a secluded, quiet spot with nearby railway links to London. So, it was near to Petersfield that they settled upon the site of over ten thousand acres.

Work was begun quickly in 1914. The stone came from Belgium and the bricks from not too far away, at Rowlands Castle. However, events from August of that year soon put a stop to the work! Building resumed after an inconvenient break, in 1919, and most of the work was completed by 1924.

Art Nouveau was passé by the time of its completion, with the new Art Deco beginning to be the style of choice.

However, its earlier, pre-war design resulted in a house that sits comfortably with the grander stately homes of England.

Some of its features were outstandingly elegant and stylish, for example the magnificent double helix design for the staircase. Had Crick and Watson discovered this, the mystery of DNA may have been solved earlier!

Despite being intimately involved with the planning and building of his country estate, once it was completed Lord Peel preferred to spend his time in London, his reason being to keep his finger on the political pulse of the nation. I can't help feeling if he'd spent a little more time in the capital, being aware of the patient's temperature in 1913, instead of house-hunting, he may well have delayed the start of his building project!

The staircase in Leydene House

So, Lady Eleanor remained in Hampshire and developed some delightful eccentricities. As a walker, I am delighted that she chose to go about her business by taking that means of transport to the neighbouring villages. When she returned home, however, she would hitch-hike, quite happy to ride in a coal truck!

One snowy winter, while she was entertaining guests, she was forced to extend their stay because the roads were blocked. Consequently, she sued nearby Petersfield Council for their failure to clear the roads for the sum of £7-17s-07d – that's £7.88 to you and me – to cover the 'the estimated cost of keeping six visitors for four days in excess of their invitation'. Unfortunately, F G Stansfield's book 'A History of East Meon' (1984) does not reveal whether she was successful in her claim. I'd like to think so, but I somehow doubt it.

Lady Eleanor Peel

The more I'm finding out about this lady, the more I'm liking her!

Whereas you or I might go to the gym for a workout, Eleanor (yes, I feel I can address her by her first name) would do her exercise regime in the morning on her balcony...nude! Ah: perhaps I wouldn't quite go that far. Employees who failed to lower their gaze quickly enough were fired on the spot.

However, there was still spying. After breakfast, Eleanor would focus a telescope upon her workers to be sure that there was no idleness.

Eleanor may have been keen to charge the council for her guests who had outstayed their welcome, but that was at just one of her parties. For about a decade, from the late 1920s, there were regular house parties in the summer and shooting parties in the winter, to which anyone who was anyone might be invited. Once, Winston Churchill – who her Ladyship described as 'a very rude man' – was a guest. I wonder if he ever got a second invitation.

These glittering years ended after her husband, Lord Peel, died in 1937, following which Lady Eleanor bought an estate near Kelso in Scotland and spent her declining years salmon fishing.

So, despite expressing reluctance when the Admiralty decided to requisition Leydene for the war effort in 1941, Eleanor was probably not too greatly worried way up North, in a remote Scottish glen with a fishing rod.

Royal Navy personnel at work at HMS Mercury

Within four months of the requisition, with most personnel accommodated in tents, Leydene was open for business as the Naval Communications School, known as the new HMS Mercury. Despite this new life for the estate ending more than twenty years ago, many local people still talk about it by that name, such was its impact on the area.

You might think that, once the war had ended, this not-really-floating-ship might have been decommissioned. Not at all! Just two years into 'The Peace', the Admiralty bought the 120 acre estate from Lady Peel for £60,000. Six years later, the remainder of the estate was sold off, sitting tenant farmers being the main buyers.

Eleanor may have retired to Scotland and eventually sold Leydene, but when she died in 1949 her remains were brought back to Hampshire for interment, and she was buried in the graveyard at All Saints' Church in the village.

However, for more than half a century, HMS Mercury had let go its anchor on the crest of the wave of the South Downs. Over the years it 'grow'd like Topsy'. By the 1960s, it was the size of a small town, with amenities so extensive it is enough to make today's town-dwellers weep with jealousy: sports facilities, recreation centre, swimming pool,

HMS Mercury from the air

cinema...and even their own pig farm (with annual profits of £2,000 supporting the sports amenities). Perhaps the piggery was an acknowledgement of Leydene's past, of Robert Peel's Tamworths, especially as the sows were named Duchess, Countess and Lady.

By the end of the 1980s, Government cuts meant that closure was imminent. Even so, The Queen and Prince Philip visited in 1991 for a garden party to celebrate its fiftieth birthday. By its sixtieth birthday, everything was closed.

With the big house split into private apartments, and some other housing created, the remaining buildings on the site have been converted for use by the Sustainability Centre, which has also taken over the grounds.

Only two questions remain: 'what became of 'the ghost of Eagle Block?' and 'what was the fate of Clarissa, the apparition from Invincible?'

A beautiful August evening near Privett

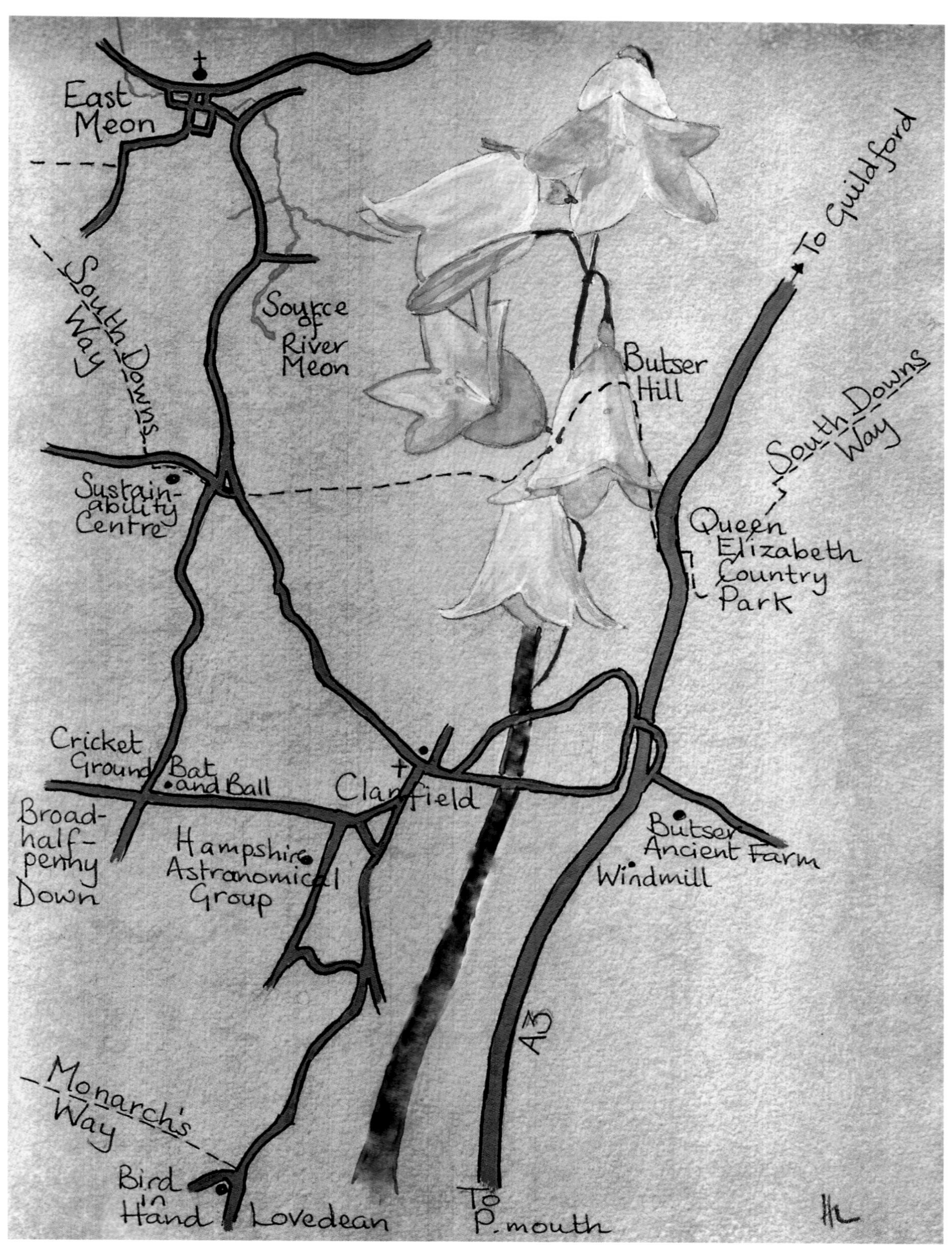
East Meon
Source of River Meon
South Downs Way
Butser Hill
To Guildford
South Downs Way
Sustainability Centre
Queen Elizabeth Country Park
Cricket Ground
Bat and Ball
Clanfield
Broadhalfpenny Down
Hampshire Astronomical Group
Butser Ancient Farm
Windmill
A3
Monarch's Way
Bird in Hand
Lovedean
To P.mouth
HL

Hambledon

Hardly will you have walked past the Sustainability Centre, when you will see a road sign to the village of Hambledon. This is a village with a church and many houses that have that chocolate-box look about them.

Towards the church in Hambledon

The reason some folk may wish to divert from their ramblings is, however, located about half-a-mile before you reach the village boundary. No, not the pub, but the cricket ground. Those who feel an affinity with the sound of leather on willow may wish to pause and contemplate the field at Broadhalfpenny Down: 'the birthplace of cricket'!

Here it was that the Hambledon Cricket Club was established, possibly about 1750, a club which was regarded as the premier team until the MCC came along in 1787.

Such was the skill to be found at Hambledon, rivals might run to extreme lengths (or widths) to increase their chances!

One of the greatest scandals was the outrageous Monster Bat incident on the 25th September, 1771 when one batsman – Thomas White – thought to guard the wicket by having a bat that was a wide as the wicket.

A monument to cricket

The Hambledon team was so furious it became necessary to rewrite the rule book. Henceforth, four and one quarter inches became the stipulated width, and before long the curved bat was abandoned in favour of the straight one that we know today. And up until this outrage, there had only been two stumps and one bail resting above them. So, to outwit the likes of Thomas White, a third stump and an extra bail were added by the good folk of Hambledon. Thus it was that Hambledon was where the cricket rule-book was first laid down.

Perhaps their moment of glory was when, in 1777, Hambledon Cricket Club beat the All England Team at Sevenoaks by an innings and 168 runs!

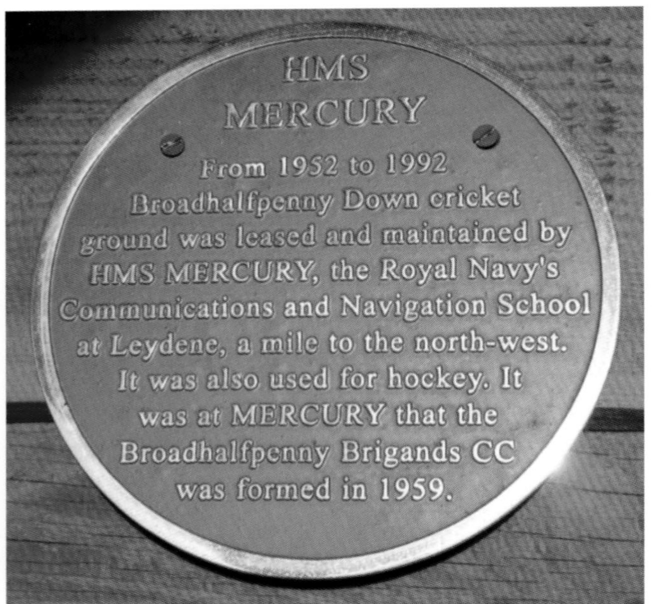

The most important cricket ground in the country? And the Royal Navy up at HMS Mercury were welcomed here too

The Bat and Ball:
Time: Gentlemen, Please!

A pub with pints and two halves

As well as for cricket, the pub opposite Broadhalfpenny Down cricket ground, The Bat and Ball, has another noteworthy tradition. The parish boundary runs straight through the middle of the building and is clearly marked upon the floor. The parishes of Clanfield and Hambledon had different licencing regulations, although in 2005 the Law abolished such discrepancies. Thus it was, when time was called on the Clanfield side of the line, the Gentlemen and players crossed over the boundary in one step to enable them to continue imbibing for a further hour.

Allegedly, women were not allowed to cross the line. Understandable, perhaps, as the little ladies might have struggled to do this safely in their petite kitten-heels!

Privett

To the glory of God...and Mammon!

If your preferred method of meditation is not sitting in a deckchair on a balmy summer's day, only disturbed by the clip of a ball or a cry of 'Howzat!', but a rather more traditional peace – with the scuffle of a church mouse, perhaps – then turn your steps back towards East Meon and onwards to the A272, beyond which, hidden in the leafy swards, is a cathedral sized church.

Like me, you might have difficulty finding the village of Privett, as the houses are spread out, rather than grouped together in a chummy huddle. However, the spire of this huge church is so grand – at 160 feet – it soars way above the tree-tops, aiding your quest.

This impressive tower can be seen for miles

At last you will find Holy Trinity Church and you too will probably marvel at its imposing size. Beneath the steeply pitched roof, the interpretation of the Gothic style is quite tasteful and uplifting.

Incongruously for such a tiny hamlet, the church seems so disproportionately large. Nowadays, with church attendance so depleted, it's not so easy for many of us to appreciate the numbers that a Victorian vicar would expect to instruct, and therefore it's hard to believe a church so huge was necessary, and that such a Victorian treasure still exists.

Perhaps it was a token of the wealth of its donor rather than spiritual need.

Now, with so few locals to create a viable congregation, its maintenance is in the hands of the Churches' Conservation Trust, a charity which does 'exactly what it says on the tin': it conserves churches.

The costs are covered by a government grant and donations from the public, but current annual outgoings exceed six million pounds, so those donations are greatly appreciated.

Founded in 1968 as the Redundant Churches Fund – it's not a very inspiring name, is it? – The Churches' Conservation Trust now preserves and maintains more than 340 churches which no longer are required for regular services, but deserve to be retained for their architectural character and beauty, as well as their focal points within communities.

The reredos behind the altar (that's a decorative panel) and the pulpit here at Holy Trinity Church are beautifully carved. Set upon Italian mosaic flooring and with impressive stained glass, I can see why Holy Trinity Church is worth preserving!

The architect, Sir Arthur Blomfield, was also involved with the building of the Royal College of Music in 1887 and also worked on the Bank of England, from 1883 until his death in 1899. As Architect to the Diocese of Winchester, he was involved in the building, maintenance and restoration of many ecclesiastic buildings in this region, including work on St Peter's in nearby Petersfield. Interestingly, before turning to literary pursuits, the young Thomas Hardy trained as a draughtsman and chose to join the practice of Blomfield in 1862.

Uplifting the Spirits!

Well, all this grandeur obviously was not cheap. Whereas the church of St John the Evangelist at West Meon cost £12,000 in 1846, just thirty years later Privett's Holy Trinity Church set back its benefactor a staggering £22,000.

So, who was this jolly-rich guy? His name was William Nicholson, Victorian MP for Petersfield.

Observant cricket fans will recognise this picture of William Nicholson from the Pavilion at the MCC (with kind permission of Nick Browne and the MCC)

Now, I think at this point I need to apologise for suggesting at the beginning of this section that this would be an escape from cricket. This is Hampshire, where cricket must be absorbed into the soul through the air, water or soil. If you've ever put 'famous people from Hampshire' into a computer search engine, you'll have noticed how nine out of ten entries seem to be cricketers!

Thus it is that I'm back to the subject again. Why? What can such a quiet place have to do with cricket? There are hardly enough houses around the church to drum up a team.

Well, it was the man responsible for this ambitiously sized church who is to blame.

Born into a gin-manufacturing family, William Nicholson played first-class cricket before becoming the MP for Petersfield, just down the road.

As the heir to the gin manufacturing family business of J & W Nicholson and Co., which produced the London Dry Gin, in 1863 he was able to buy the local stately pile of Basing Park and, like many another wealthy Victorian, he chose to build cottages for the estate workers. Although the village of Privett already existed, he commissioned many houses as well as a replacement church, creating quite a substantial settlement.

A close-up inspection will show the detail

The buildings, designed by Arthur Blomfield (1829-1899), were in in a style that became known as the 'Nicholson Style', with – like the church – steeply pitched roofs, gables and flint walls with orangey-red brick dressings.

Not surprisingly, East Hampshire District Council designated this scattered village as a Conservation area, including nine listed buildings, at the turn of this century. It is defined as 'an area of special architectural or historical interest, the character of which it is desirable to preserve or enhance'. It is also part of an Area of Outstanding Natural Beauty.

All these grand titles are a convincing reason why William Nicholson's little housing project is worth a diversion.

The village maintained its importance locally right up until the late 1950s, helped by having its own railway station from 1903 until 1955. Since then, with the closure of the school in 1970 hastening its decline, the village has quietly taken a back-foot in the life of Hampshire.

Now a private house: Privett Railway Station

But back to Mr Nicholson. Obviously, the drinking of gin (by other people) did him no harm whatsoever.

He had time on his hands to be a 'gentleman' which, as any cricket aficionado knows, was someone who had time to dedicate to the sport as an amateur – unpaid but not without skill.

He appears to have been a talented all-rounder, as his obituary stated: 'as a wicket keeper...standing up pluckily to the fastest bowling...an exceedingly fast runner between wickets, a capital judge of a short run, and altogether an energetic player.'

He obviously loved the game and was a member of the MCC for many years. His money was also very much appreciated by the club.

Whereas Mr Ward gave Lord's Cricket Ground £5,000 in 1825 (when Thomas Lord was on a sticky wicket) to save the club, William Nicholson stumped up £18,333-6s-8d, enabling the club to buy the freehold of the ground. Future donations included £10,000 – almost half of the cost – of the famous pavilion in 1889.

The Pavilion at Lord's Cricket Ground (with kind permission of the MCC)

But let's not forget: William Nicholson was a wily businessman, and of course the donations were really loans. The 1866 one was at five percent interest, which – even if it was a simple interest repayment and not compounded or an annual rate – means that in that one 'donation' he made a profit of £916-12s-4d. That's in the region of one and a half million today.

According to the history of J & W Nicholson and Co., shortly after his generosity to the club, the MCC adopted the well-known red and golden-yellow colours, which co-incidentally are the colours of the label for Nicholson's Dry London Gin!

No contemporary records have been found to corroborate this claim, although the MCC itself does give credence to the assertion. The 'egg and bacon' colours of the MCC were first used in that decade and were probably a 'thank you' to Nicholson and, although many a Victorian would have frowned upon such a commercial sponsorship deal, business is business!

Welcome to East Hampshire. We're Safely Obscure

The Road to Little Dribbling; Bill Bryson

On his travels through Britain for his sequel to 'Notes from a Small Island', Bill Bryson chanced upon the ghost of the Meon Valley Railway line on its route between Alton and Gosport. He also discovered its place in history at Droxford, as I described earlier.

Here at Privett the line's arrival and departure had dramatic effects upon the size of the village. This recently built village benefitted from the advantages of a transport link to the outside world, bringing trade and prosperity, and thrived. However, the closure of the line to passengers in 1955 and freight in 1968 meant a drastic decline in Privett's fortunes and why Holy Trinity Church seems so extraordinarily large compared to the size of the community. The dates show us that the line was doomed long before the Beeching Report, so we cannot place the blame on Dr Richard Beeching's attempts to rationalise our loss making national network.

Much of the old line has been turned into a footpath, and the result is a tree-lined, sunlight-dappled track, which is easy walking as it is fairly flat. The rails have gone and much of the paraphernalia has gone – no water hopper or coke bunkers. The bridges, however, still duck and dive across the landscape. These impressed Bill Bryson with their careful brickwork, banded with colour.

For all you trainspotters, these are pictures of East Tisted Station, the next one up the line. Also now a private house, the 'garden' is a train in the station, as well as some of the other station bits and pieces.

The station at Privett is still there and, like the other few remaining buildings, is now a private house. Like the bridges, the planners aimed to make these attractive and to give an aura of history and timelessness by hinting at times past in their design.

Nearby to Privett Station is The Angel, an hotel on the A32. Formerly called The Privett Bush, in its day it was not unknown for train drivers to nip across the road for a swift pint while their train was waiting at the platform!

I wonder, had the line lasted, if Bill Bryson's slogan for East Hampshire might have been less appropriate. Would the survival of those long-lost railways have taken away the pressure on our road infrastructure? If freight had been transported by rail, the traffic flow on the roads might have been smoother, opening up the county. In this parallel universe, perhaps a Mr Perks would welcome you to your station as you arrived to collect the goods ordered over the internet, instead of finding a card on your mat informing you that you were not in, and the new television lobbed over the garden gate by the van driver.

Perhaps the county's slogan could have been: 'Welcome to East Hampshire. We're reassuringly conspicuous'.

Lazing on a Sunday Afternoon

Midway between Privett and Hambledon, these two locations of historical note for cricket aficionados, lies East Meon, you'll have realised, which has its own present-day cricket team. For lovers of the game, how better than to while away a sunny Sunday afternoon than by cheering on East Meon Cricket Club as they triumph over a rival team?

But do be careful! One of the original rules stated "Persons of known profligate character, intoxicated persons and beggars shall be excluded from the ground." Now, having met the team in the local pub, I'm sure that this has been maintained for the players. However, I'd hate to think that any visiting spectators might be turned away.

Clanfield

Clanfield is another of those villages that the South Downs Way twists and turns its way past, like a centre-forward dribbling round the goalie! However, it does have several shops which can make it a very useful diversion for those of you needing to stock up on supplies for your journey.

The late Victorian church, St James, is in the centre. The flint work on the outside creates a deceptive look, but once inside the warmth of brick and tile work wraps over you, comfortingly.

Green bin added!

Nearby is the old village well, intriguingly covered by a thatched roof. Although it is fronted by a useful bus stop, it is the idiotic locating of a green rubbish bin right next to one of the uprights that amazes me most!

Instant Pub!

If the bin upsets you too much, it may be necessary to sit down to recover in the nearby pub, The Rising Sun. In its present incarnation, it is quite new, having been rebuilt in 2004, although, like the church, its flint exterior gives the initial impression of a much older building.

The present incarnation of The Rising Sun

However, the previous pub, on the same site, also could not lay claim to any great antiquity. That didn't last even fifty years. It is, however, notable for the speed of its erection. By 1960 the even older building had seen better days and needed replacing. Licencing laws at the time were such that, had a period of twenty-four hours gone by without a drink being sold, then the landlord would have needed to re-apply, which would have been very tedious. To prevent this, it was decided to get the newly built pub up and into use in just one day!

Work started seriously at sunrise – five o'clock – on Tuesday, 24th May, 1960, and by quarter-past eleven that morning the whole structure was in place. The rest of the day was spent installing the fixtures and fittings.

At six o'clock in the evening, at the time any other pub would have been opening for the evening, the first pint was drawn!

At the time, this was certainly of note for the five-year-old the 'Guinness Book of Records'. That building has now gone and the current pub, which has been there for more than a decade, took a little longer to build and looks quite sturdy!

We have seen the seven stars

Henry IV, part ii; Wm. Shakespeare

I'm sure, for many of us, the most serious that we've ever been about astronomy is "Star Trek". What is even more worrying, is that for others the acme of their space knowledge is the comedy series "Red Dwarf"! The good news is there are some people who are more advanced in such matters, even if these matters are dark matters!

At Clanfield you will find the home of the Hampshire Astronomical Group. It is an extremely active society, with regular meetings, courses and open-days. If you are lucky, your visit may coincide with one of these events. The group was founded over fifty years ago, although it didn't move to its present site until the 1970s, after several other relocations.

Exploring strange new worlds ... The Great Nebula in Orion, also known as M42!

(Courtesy of Simon Downs, member of the Hampshire Astronomical Group)

One of its earlier moves (in 1963) was the result of light pollution, when too much ambient lighting obscures the view. It's rather like driving your car at night and the passenger is using a torch to read the map: even if it does not cause an accident, it is very frustrating! And whereas you can ask the passenger to switch it off, it is not so easy to get all the street-lights off, impossible to get car head-lights removed and an absolute no-hoper to get everyone to close their curtains!

Even the major observatories have suffered: the Royal Observatory left its home at Greenwich in the 1950s for the leafier lanes of rural East Sussex...and even that location became too polluted over subsequent years, so they were forced to move again.

Clanfield is quite remote and as the members have invested a great deal in the centre, including new and better technology, it is to be hoped the bright lights of the ever-growing cities can be kept at bay!

Although the Hampshire Astronomical Group is essentially amateur, it's no bad thing! The enthusiasm of hobbyists often shows a dedication, knowledge and skill that is equal to all but the best professionals, partly because it is not just 'a job'. Many of us have our own specialisms and interests where we know this to be true.

Indeed, the work done by the group is recognised by the International Minor Planet Centre in the USA and, perhaps of even more importance to us Brits, was visited by the late Sir Patrick Moore!

One of the group's major concerns is with comets, and they are currently of great interest as space scientists attempt to explore them and to examine samples taken from these phenomena as they continue on their travels. So maybe a visit to one of their events will add an extra dimension to your walk!

Pompey the Great

Follow the road South out of Clanfield for a couple of miles to find the village of Lovedean, on the northern fringes of Portsmouth. Here you will find The Bird in Hand public house. Now a thriving pub/restaurant, in the middle of the 20th century it was a much more rural location and the ancient building had a thatched roof, which would have added to its charm by today's standards.

The Bird in Hand at Lovedean

But it was at the time of the Second World War that it had its role in sporting history. Kept quiet then, and largely forgotten now, it was the proud home of the FA Cup! So much for the boasts of the Manchester United Red Devils or the Chelsea or Arsenal fans; Portsmouth can boast that it has held the FA Cup for more consecutive years than any other club!

Portsmouth beat Wolverhampton Wanderers by four goals to one in 1939 to be awarded the cup into their care. Along came the war and the FA Cup competition was abandoned for 'the Duration'. At first, it was kept in the city at Fratton Park, but fear of bomb damage meant the manager, Jack Tinn, needed somewhere safer for it.

A friend of Mr Tinn was the father of the then landlord of The Bird, as it was known at the time, and it was agreed the cup would be much safer there. For most of the time it was kept underneath the landlord's bed, although occasionally it made an appearance, during which time it was not unheard of for it to have been used as a very large drinking vessel!

Once the war was over, the FA Cup competition resumed. Personally, I am really glad they looked after it well, so that it was nice 'n' shiny for my team to pick up in 1947!

As they say: a bird in the hand is worth two in the bush, so being the holders of the FA Cup for seven consecutive years is a claim unlikely to be challenged by any other club.

If, however, you are cheering on your team as they collect the trophy next May, I am sorry to disappoint you: it isn't the same one. Even by the 1940s, the Football Association was on trophy number three. Since then it has been replaced twice. By 1992 that trophy was over eighty years old and not as sturdy as it had been in its youth. An identical one was produced, but that too has now seen better days and a similar design, but a little larger, has graced the trophy cabinets of winners since 2014.

Absolutely champion! The FA Cup on the bar

Butser Hill and Queen Elizabeth Country Park

Well, let's stop this shilly-shallying and get back to our expedition along the South Downs Way.

A recent view of the A3, looking towards Butser Hill

As you turn at the top of Butser Hill, at 889 feet high, the highest chalk ridge on the South Downs, the landscape swoops away to the South, providing a panorama of wide open verdant sward, cut through with a snake of traffic belting up and down the A3. It is one of England's Marilyns: meaning that it has a drop of 492 feet or more all the way around.

A deep cutting through the landscape enables vehicles to progress without a steep climb. In times gone by, travellers had to clamber to the heights of Butser as they journeyed between London and beyond down to the South Coast at Portsmouth.

... and a newspaper cutting of the same view about a century ago

Nicholas Nickleby, the eponymous hero of Charles Dickens' novel, made this journey and, despite the struggle of the ascent, the traffic-free view was obviously stunning for the wayfarer coming across it for the first time:

> Onward they kept, with steady purpose, and entered at length upon a wide and spacious tract of downs, with every variety of little hill and plain to change their verdant surface. Here, there shot up, almost perpendicularly, into the sky, a height so steep, as to be hardly accessible to any but the sheep and goats that fed upon its sides,...Hills swelling above each other; and undulations shapely and uncouth, smooth and rugged, graceful and grotesque, thrown negligently side by side, bounded the view in each direction...
>
> By degrees, the prospect receded more and more on either hand, and as they had been shut out from rich and extensive scenery, so they emerged once again upon the open country...the way had been difficult...they turned off the path to the door of a roadside inn, yet twelve miles short of Portsmouth.
>
> 'Is it a good road?' inquired Nicholas.
>
> 'Very bad,' said the landlord. As of course, being a landlord, he would say.
>
> 'I want to get on,' observed Nicholas, hesitating. 'I scarcely know what to do.'
>
> 'Don't let me influence you,' rejoined the landlord. 'I wouldn't go on if it was me.'
>
> Nicholas Nickleby; Chapter 22; Charles Dickens

Milestone at the Southern side of the hill (actually at the visitors' centre of the QEII Park) of the type that Nicholas would have encountered on his journey

Unfortunately, the inn at the bottom where Nicholas and Smike were welcomed by the landlord and were introduced to the wonderful Vincent Crummles is no longer there. The modern equivalent welcome that you'll get is a baguette at the Visitor Centre at the Queen Elizabeth Country Park.

Mountain bikers can enjoy the hills at the QEII Park

Yes: the Queen Elizabeth Country Park is one of those lovely places with a café and toilets. It covers 1,400 acres and is largely a wooded area, with plenty of things to do for children and families.

The countryside and wildlife are well managed for the visitor, with even car parking for the day-tripper, and there is much to keep you occupied, from leisurely picnics to tearing around on mountain bikes.

Walkers with children will probably appreciate a few hours here. Huge beech trees, many around eighty years old, tower overhead as you stroll through its glades. As the South Downs Way goes right through the middle, even a short break is a good idea, although hikers keen to get on to their next destination can pick up leaflets to encourage their return, but then put their best foot forward and continue on their way.

Much-welcomed markers along the way for map-readers like me!

Just like Old Winchester Hill, the custodians of this area have signposted lots of their own footpaths, which can make it difficult to find the one that you actually need, as the Ordnance Survey map makes no sense here. Several times I needed to back-track, as I found I was on the path back to where I had come from. Fellow travellers were as baffled as I was. In the end, I went off-piste just to get back to where I should have been. If you are heading to Eastbourne, just remember that that is onwards and upwards!

Holey Smoke!

Early morning at the ancient village settlement (courtesy of Butser Ancient Farm)

Just to the South of the Country Park, but within the South Downs National Park, is Butser Ancient Farm. This is an experimental site to test archeological theories.

It was originally constructed near to the top of Butser Hill, by the Council for British Archaeology, in 1970, but after a couple of moves it's now at the bottom of the hill, on the opposite side of the A3 (no, it was relocated: it didn't just slide to the bottom of Butser on a whim!), on the road to Chalton.

Overlooking Butser Ancient Farm, towards the QEII Park

Reconstructions take place at this site to find out how Ancient Britons lived and worked, based on evidence found on archaeological digs and research. As it is impossible to ask the people who were there, practical experiments take place to verify or disprove what is assumed.

For example, I can't be the only one who remembers from my schooldays how ancient folk definitely had a hole at the top of their roundhouses to let out the smoke from their fires. They definitely did: I definitely remember copying the diagram from the book!

Ah! No! Got that wrong! If you try that, the heat will go up and out, but the smoke stubbornly stays. What is worse is that sparks from the fire will be drawn up to roof and will set fire to it!

So, if you don't have a hole in the roof, won't everyone suffocate to death? Well, no! Firstly, without the up-draft it is possible to control the fire more effectively.

Secondly, the smoke works its way out through the thatch at the top, and the only things that get suffocated are the bugs. So, the smoke escapes, the fire can be controlled, residents are still alive, bugs are exterminated, birds no longer peck at the thatch trying to get a meal from the bugs and the roof lasts longer. A win-win-win-win-win-win situation!

Visitors are welcome to the centre, where they can find out about living conditions and farming from the Stone Age right through to Anglo Saxon times. If you want to go further into this living history research, then as you continue towards Eastbourne, soon after entering Sussex, there is the Weald and Downland Open Air Museum at Singleton!

Oh, and another point to shatter all your beliefs from your primary school days: it wasn't all roundhouses. While most of Britain went round in circles, in mainland Europe people were a lot more 'square': their houses were likely to be rectangular.

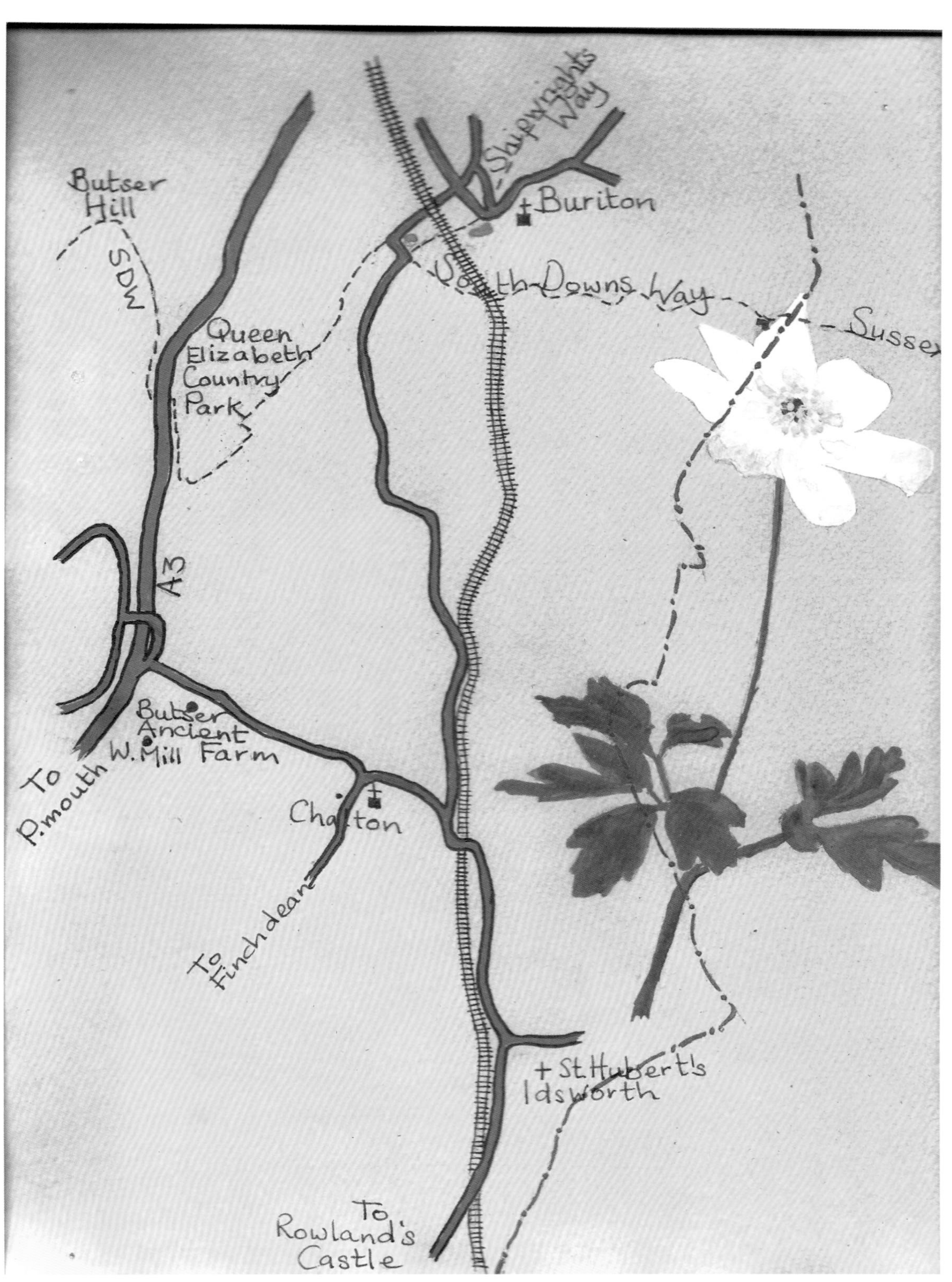
Shipwrights Way
Butser Hill
Buriton
SDW
South Downs Way
Sussex
Queen Elizabeth Country Park
A3
Butser Ancient Farm
W. Mill
To P.mouth
Chalton
To Finchdean
St. Hubert's Idsworth
To Rowland's Castle

Chalton

From the visitor centre at the Queen Elizabeth Country Park, you can pick up the Staunton Way which winds its way southwards towards the village of Chalton, little more than two miles away.

Nowadays, although several roads cross through the village (among them to places like Idsworth, Buriton and Clanfield), the hum of traffic is more likely to be from farm machinery than from the heavy-good vehicles and family cars which bounce along the A3 just off to the West.

At one time, in its earliest Saxon days, even the farm-land noise would have been made up of the horse and plough, and the animals calling to each other. All these would have been part of the demesne of the Lord of the Manor, who may have bought the land, or been given it by the king as a reward. Buying a manor was an investment – adding to the lord's income, power and prestige.

Among the various Lords of this manor, in Mediaeval times, was Simon de Montfort, who inherited it. A thorn in the side of King Henry III, he strove to limit the power of the monarchy and is credited with being the founder of Parliament.

Like many other villages, the most prominent buildings in Chalton are the pub and the church. There is, however, a stronger link between these two than just post-service refreshment. Long before it became The Red Lion, the building provided lodgings for the craftsmen who came to build St Michael's Church.

What history might these walls have seen?

Reputedly the oldest pub in Hampshire, The Red Lion itself did not come into existence as an inn until the early sixteenth century. It would be lovely to imagine Henry VIII drowning in his cups, propping up the bar, following the sinking of his favourite ship, the Mary Rose, visible just down the road at Portsmouth – but that is just me day-dreaming. Something, however, must have upset a rather mischievous ghost who enjoys tampering with the gas taps for the beer! I suppose that a phantom is one way to ensure that your pint is chilled. Sadly, no-one knows who this shade is or why it is there.

It may be hard to believe, but this sleepy little village once stood on the main road from London to Portsmouth. Indeed, until the introduction of the toll-road, the precursor to the A3, this was one of the scariest parts of the journey, with thieves and highwaymen most likely to accost you!

Stepping back in time

It was the best of roads, it was the worst of roads...

In Charles Dickens' description of the journey from London to Portsmouth taken by Nicholas Nickleby, the landlord of the inn to the south of Butser Hill was very discouraging towards Nicholas's wish to continue onwards:

'I want to get on,' observed Nicholas, hesitating. 'I scarcely know what to do.'
'Don't let me influence you,' rejoined the landlord. 'I wouldn't go on if it was me.'

Nicholas Nickleby; Chapter 22; Charles Dickens

This may have been a ploy to delay a customer for profit, but poor Nicholas was unlikely to put much into the inn's coffers. It's more likely it was a wise caution about the onward journey.

Back in the nineteenth century, the current A3 was no more important than several other options that splay their way like a river delta through the landscape. Nicholas's landlord may have been prudent to alert travellers and probably to offer advice depending upon the weather and known criminals in the area: the area was feared for its robbers!

But it was also the state of the road surfaces which, like these days, was a cause for consternation.

If, like me, you've had to buy a new wheel for the car as a result of pothole damage, you may think things could not have been much worse then. Oh, yes they could! In the past, roads were often little more than oft-used footpaths that were considered the best route to somewhere and thus widened over the years.

Think of a footpath used by walkers these days, following heavy rain and squidged about by boots, walking poles, horses, bicycles, bikes, quad-bikes, off-roaders, farm vehicles and...well: need I go on? Our main roads were often in a similar or even worse condition, which meant that any journey could be very uncomfortable, long and distressing.

Perhaps a highwayman was the only way to perk things up!

So, in centuries past a traveller's choice of route would often be determined by the weather, the foot-pads or even why he was travelling in the first place.

At least our intrepid traveller would know how much further he had to go to reach his destination: in the 1750s a law was passed, declaring that milestones should be erected along the way stating the miles to the major towns along the route. Occasionally a stone marker can still be found nestling in long grass. Later ones were made of cast iron.

You may have enjoyed reading C J Sansom's Tudor detective novels. If so, you will remember that in 'Heartstone' Shardlake and his companions join a troop of soldiers heading for Portsmouth. In clement July weather they make good progress from London at about fifteen miles each day.

Several days into their journey they camp overnight outside Buriton. It would appear that their chosen route avoided the hill at Butser, probably because of the carts of heavy military equipment they had with them. The next day, just two miles further southwards, a broken cartwheel resulted in a long delay of several hours for all the following carts (Ha! Makes you think of the M25, doesn't it?).

So, this helps to illustrate how roads in the area of Chalton were an alarming part of anyone's journey!

Although this may be a fictional account, it does reflect the reality of travel in times past!

The Portsmouth road was called The Road to Assassination in the early nineteenth century as there were so many murders committed along the way. In the late seventeenth century, the route was renowned for smuggling too – brandy in, wool out. Such was the level of crime, the journey was not for the faint-hearted. In an endeavour to intimidate the villains, gibbets were set up alongside the road, with the executed baddies left hanging and swaying in the breeze. How much these corpses deterred the felons we can only guess, but I feel certain that these creaking corpses made the journey even more terrifying for the travellers.

The Whirligig of Time

Twelfth Night: Wm. Shakespeare

I'm sure we've all winced as, once more, our car has lurched into yet another pothole, and it is little consolation to be told that it used to be worse in the good old days.

It was in the middle of the sixteen hundreds that the Government decided that action was needed to improve the conditions on our ghastly roads. So private enterprise, as we would call it these days, was seen as the answer. The Turnpike or Toll Road was invented. Investors would form companies which would raise money to build and maintain good roads, and then people would be charged to use them until the costs had been recovered. After that, obviously, travellers would use them freely. Of course not! As we can see with modern examples of tolls, the charges didn't stop and the investors continued to get returns on their capital.

But don't think these roads made everything hunky-dory for travellers! In the early days, travelling was still a precarious activity, what with crime, road accidents or simply suffering a severe chill if you could only afford to sit atop the coach. It was not uncommon for people to write their wills before their departure. If their journey was too bad, they worried, it might mean their departure from this life too!

Tempers could easily fray with the stress of the journey, as a toll collector at Sheet Bridge near Petersfield found out. An angry traveller wounded the poor man on the arm with a sword. Luckily, he survived this early example of Turnpike Rage!

The good news for travellers was that roads began to improve. With civil engineering progress, and people like Thomas Telford (as the eighteenth century turned into the nineteenth) and John Loudon McAdam (in about 1820) new methods and products meant roads began to improve. And then the railways came. And then fewer people and goods were transported by road. And then the toll companies went bust. And then laws were passed so that councils would take over the maintenance and the expense. And then there were potholes!

Well, I Declare!

From the top of Butser Hill, as you looked across the valley, with the traffic on the A3 glinting (I hope) in brilliant sunshine, you will have seen – high on a hill directly to the south of you – the top of Chalton Windmill just peeking through the trees. The fixed traditional sails are without slats, but as it's not used as a windmill these days their absence may be missed visually, although with the strong winds that can blow across the area, it seems a lot safer for the structure of the building.

Right there: the windmill atop the hill

The present structure is from the nineteenth century, although there were records of a windmill on this site from mediaeval times. Like many agricultural and industrial buildings which outlive their time, it became derelict. Had it not attained listed status in 1954, it would have been demolished. Following restoration and its incorporation into a newly built house, it's now a private home.

Nevertheless, the walk towards the windmill across the fields from Chalton is lovely and it affords panoramic views of the surrounding countryside and even on to Portsmouth and beyond.

An Open and Shut(ter) Case?

Not far into your journey from Winchester, you passed by Telegraph Hill, a proposed shutter signalling station on the messaging route between London and Plymouth. Chalton had a similar station on the line between London and Portsmouth, which by then had been converted to using semaphore.

Allegedly, this line was responsible for a financial crash in 1815. Nevertheless, despite being a lovely story, it is just that: a story. It was said, following Wellington's victory over Napoleon at Waterloo, the good news was received in Portsmouth and an eagerly awaited report was relayed to the Admiralty in London.

The result demonstrated the unreliability of the signalling system, especially in inclement weather. For a start, we know that icy conditions could render the shutters inoperable.

A poorly composed message and bad weather supposedly combined to create chaos. The message was supposed to read "Wellington defeated Napoleon at Waterloo . . ." Unfortunately, fog descended after just two words had been sent. As a result of this foreshortened message, there was turmoil at the Stock Exchange (as one of those 'black' days we occasionally hear about erupted) on the misapprehension that Napoleon had been victorious.

So that's that, then.

However...

Sunday, 18th June, 1815: in what is now Belgium, a battle lasting many hours was fought, resulting in the defeat of Napoleon Bonaparte.

Anxiously, London waited. Meanwhile, Rosthchild family couriers moved around freely in war-torn Europe. One – John Bothworth – travelled speedily to his boss – Nathan Rothschild – with news of the victory. Loyally, Nathan rushed to the Prime Minister, the Earl of Liverpool, to inform him. But as this was contrary to what the Government supposed to have happened, he was not believed.

"This hiking is really hard work!"

Certain enough of his version of events, Nathan's dealers on the Stock Exchange began openly to sell their shares, generating enough panic so that others sold their stock too, resulting in prices plummeting. Before the truth got out and the market could rally, Nathan's agents then discreetly bought as much as they could at the lowest of prices. The government officially found out who was really the victor at Waterloo when Major Henry Percy arrived with Wellington's dispatch late on the 21st June: time enough for Nathan to do well from his information. It is said he got a return of twenty to one on his investment!

If nothing else, the need for an accurate and speedy means of conveying military messages was apparent. These days we might frown on what happened as 'insider dealing', but really it is rather like telling your gran that it was Colonel Mustard in the library with the candlestick, and Gran still insisting on Miss Scarlet/study/rope. You've done your best to help her, been ignored and then won for yourself. In his shoes, what would you have done?

Rowlands Castle

If your walk is ending at the Hampshire border, you may have some time to explore the area before you leave. Petersfield is to the North, but southwards there are a few places worth a look-see, including Portsmouth with its dockyard.

You may not be ending your walk, as the route continues into West Sussex, but – especially if you have children with you – a day of doing something different may appeal.

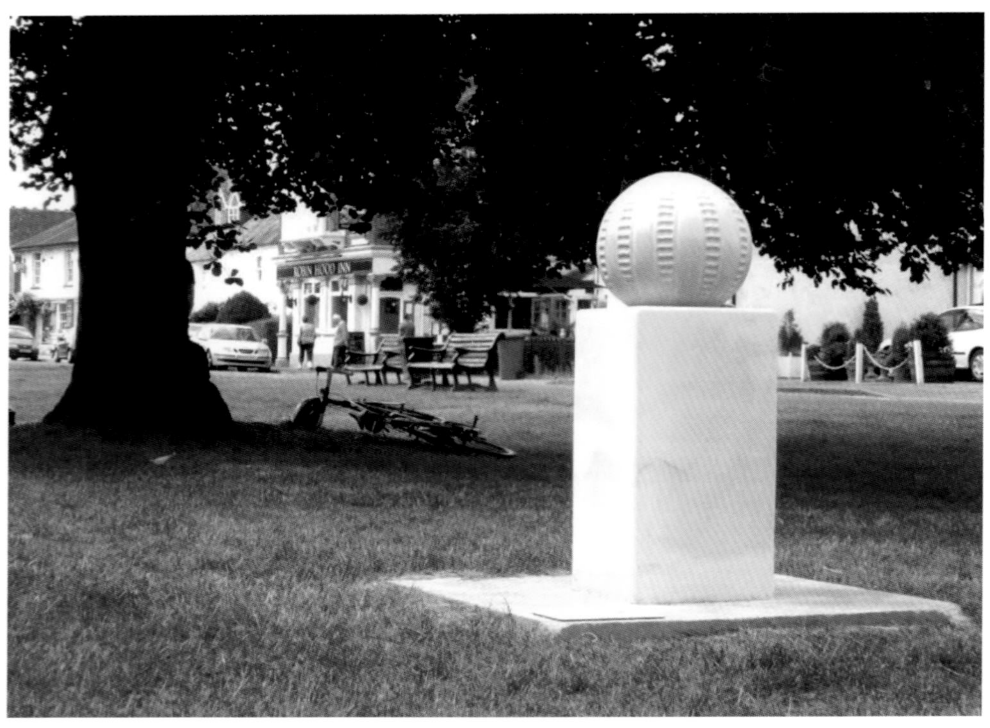

A marker for the Shipwrights' Way: a shepherd's crown, fossilised sea-urchins, often dug up by farmers in the fields

The railway can take you from Petersfield into Portsmouth. If you are driving, there are a few calling-off points (a pub, a church and a small town) on the way. However, it is probably less stressful to take the train, and the station is close-by the Historic Dockyard.

On the way, one of the calling-off points is a small town called Rowlands Castle, a name that conjures up Arthurian thoughts, a hint of a fairy story or even Robert Browning. The truth is somewhat more prosaic: it's a commuter town, with a railway

station giving access to Portsmouth, Petersfield and London, and good links to the motorway system.

Alternatively, if you are travelling to Portsmouth, you could park at Rowlands Castle and take the train from there.

The railway was also used for freight in its earlier days, bringing more employment and wealth to the area.

From ancient times, vast deposits of local clay were the foundation of the town's development, with the Romans creating pottery, and the industry continued over the centuries.

With the better transport links following the arrival of the railway, brick making became a large industry because these bricks were in great demand as London underwent a massive expansion in late-Victorian times. Those belts of suburban terraces surrounding the capital cried out for Rowlands Castle's produce. Eventually, the clay ran out and the industry foundered, but not before Leydene House at East Meon had had its share in the 1920s.

The sight of cake always gives me a warm feeling: a homely café by the village green

It is now a quiet, tranquil place, with a large 'village green' and several places for refreshment! Indeed, time your journey right as you come back from 'naval' gazing in Portsmouth, and you could fit in a cream tea hard-by the village green!

One other thing may catch your eye as you pass by, at the intersection of the B2148 and the B2149 there is a discrete monument to Rowland Castle's 'Agincourt' moment: whereas King Henry V did his big bit further along the coast to the West, King George VI did his version, reviewing the troops as they went off for the D-Day landings in Normandy.

Crookley Pool at Horndean, not far from Rowlands Castle, is another of those wonderful gardens open under the National Garden scheme. It has areas of formality, but still manages to feel like a cottage garden. Certainly, this is a place for gardeners to while away an hour or two.

Portsmouth

A visit to Portsmouth Historic Dockyard would certainly keep everyone occupied for the day, as there is a lot to see (and even the opportunity for some shopping at the outlet centre next door).

I Saw Three Ships...

HMS Victory's rigging

Most famously, there is Nelson's flag-ship HMS Victory, and also King Henry VIII's pride and joy – The Mary Rose. Also, there is the Royal Navy's first iron ship, HMS Warrior, from the time of Queen Victoria.

I feel it is my duty at this point to do my bit for my home town and make it clear that Portsmouth Dockyard may claim ownership of Nelson's flagship, but it was actually built at Chatham Dockyard in Kent!

Also, Portsmouth is lucky to have it as it very nearly never left Chatham!

9½...Inches

No, this is not a mistype of a film title, it's the near-miss concerning the launch of HMS Victory at Chatham! The night before the launch, Hartly Larkin (the foreman responsible for effecting a successful departure) realised that the Victory – the largest ship that had ever been built for the Royal Navy – was too large to get through the gates! After checking the measurements in the morning, Larkin's fears were confirmed:

at its largest point the vessel was nine and a half inches too wide to pass through to the river.

He went to his boss, who began to panic. This was unhelpful, as the poor man suffered from "violent and frequent attacks of a bilious disorder of the bowels".

However, Mr Larkin took control of the situation by asking for the help of the shipwrights who "hacked away at the parts of the open gate" before the tide rose inside the dock and the Victory began to float.

Two years later, Hartly Larkin wrote to the Navy Board requesting financial remuneration for his efforts on that day, but his request was ignored! In that letter he used the phrase "and then the tide flowed some time": not at the point in his account when the ship was successfully afloat, but when recalling telling his boss of the problem. So maybe the tide that flowed was not the one on the River Medway!

However, Portsmouth is the place to go if you want to explore Nelson's Flag-ship!

Hooray and Up She Rises!

What Shall We Do with the Drunken Sailor?; trad.

It was, however, The Mary Rose that grabbed my attention first. She was King Henry VIII's pride and joy but sank upon leaving Portsmouth Harbour in 1545, before she could engage in battle with the French. Nearly all the crew were lost: they were trapped under the netting which had been used to prevent the enemy from boarding!

The enormous project of raising her from the seabed in 1982 and, following that, the decades of treatment required to prevent her from crumbling into dust, is amazing! It's not just the ship herself: it is the archaeological work upon the skeletons of the sailors and the detritus of their lives which is so fascinating.

Bottom-right - The ship on display while still undergoing preservation. Top and bottom-left images (courtesy the Mary Rose Trust) - years of treatment for the timbers have now ended and she is displayed in all her glory.

A Riveting Addition?

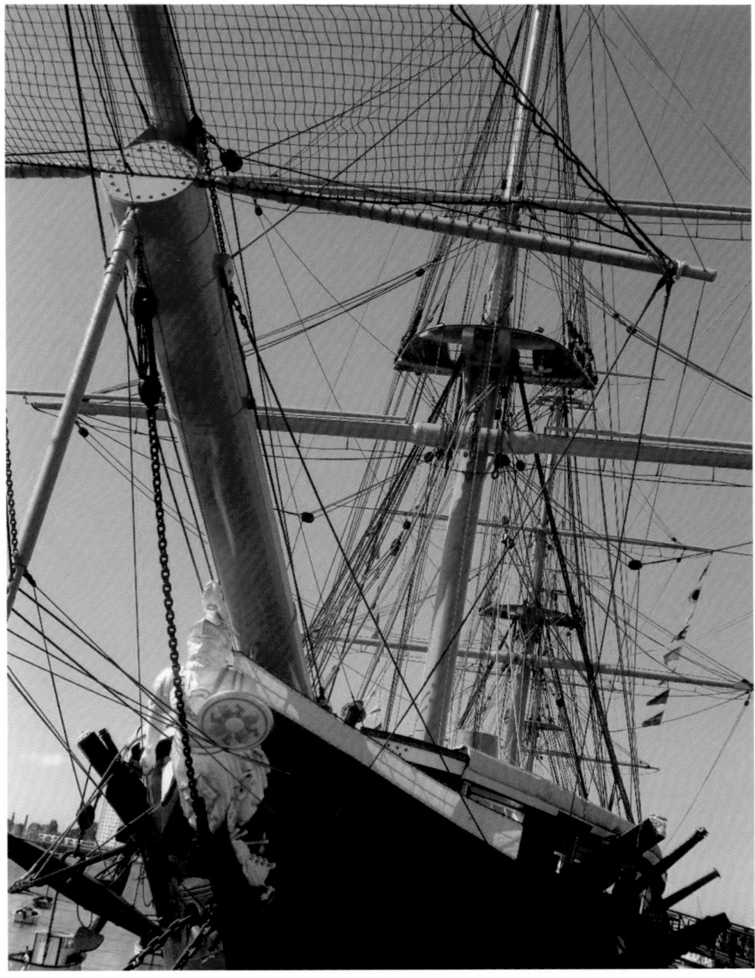
HMS Warrior

The Dockyard also has a much more modern ship: HMS Warrior, the Royal Navy's first iron ship, built to keep ahead of the game in the sea-race against the French. Although I would not be surprised if the work of Isambard Kingdom Brunel had an influence upon the design, he had died in 1859 and was not involved in the project. Co-incidentally, the great man himself was born in Portsmouth in 1806.

When Warrior was commissioned in 1861, she was the biggest, best and fastest ship in the fleet, powered by both sail and steam.

However, as a portent of the throw-away culture of the future, she was downgraded only ten years later, as upgrades and innovations were introduced to newer vessels.

By 1883 she was 'placed on reserve' and in 1923 she was put up for sale as scrap. It is worth noting, although we regard The Mary Rose as a lady with a life

On-board this lovely vessel

cut short, she was in active service for thirty-four-years – half as long again as Warrior – before being submerged beneath the waves.

HMS Victory was in active service for forty-seven years before being relegated from the top rank, and was already a grand old lady of forty in 1805 when she starred in the Battle of Trafalgar, as Lord Nelson's flag-ship. It is indeed the pairing of the two which has become iconic in our history.

The Captain's cabin on The Victory

The famous painting of Horatio Nelson's death, by Arthur William Davis, which can be seen at the National Maritime Museum in Greenwich, is one of many depictions of the scene on the Victory. Although they generally portray him close by Vice-Admiral Hardy, there is some doubt that his fellow officer was actually there, although there were eye-witnesses to confirm he was. So we'll never really know the truth about whether Nelson said "Kiss me Hardy"!

HMS Victory carried the body of Nelson back to England. He was placed in a casket which was then filled with brandy to preserve the body for its long journey. The Victory berthed at Chatham (yes, that's another one in the eye for Portsmouth!) where an autopsy was performed, after which Nelson's remains were moved on towards Greenwich before interment at Saint Paul's Cathedral. Strangely, I understand, after his repatriation, when the casket was opened, the brandy had gone!

As an aside, the sarcophagus used for Nelson at St Paul's was not just second-hand, it was third hand. It was commissioned for Cardinal Wolsey, but after he fell from grace King Henry VIII purloined it for himself. However, it was still incomplete at the time he died (and I wonder: would he have fitted?). So, King George III donated it for Nelson!

So, three ships, each with its own special history, to fill your day. There is no denying that it is an expensive day out, especially if there is a group of you. If you are likely to be in the area in the following months, then you can get better value, as the entry ticket is valid for a year.

Words, Words, Words...

This scept'red isle...This fortress built by nature...This precious stone set in the silver sea...Yes, well, let's not get too carried away here. The point is, Britain has a very long coastline which not only acts as a ginormous moat, it also means that its people have a strong link with the sea. So it isn't surprising that many of our figures of speech have their roots in our seafaring history. A few minutes on the computer can explain many everyday phrases. There are far too many to be mentioned here, but some examples can seem obvious, once you think about it.

Here goes!

Our phrase	How we use it these days	Where it comes from
Above board	*Something that is plain to see, is honest.*	*Something that is up on deck for all to see.*
Bail out	*Helping out someone in difficulty.*	*Helping to prevent a boat from sinking by removing the water.*
Clean bill of health	*The doctor has said that you are not ill.*	*A Bill of Health was issued to a ship leaving port, stating that there was no infection or epidemic aboard (or at the port from which it was leaving) at the time of its departure.*
Clean slate	*Making a fresh start, forgetting what may have happened previously.*	*Courses and distances were recorded on a slate. At the end of a watch, the slate would be wiped clean as the new watch began its duty.*
Copper-bottomed	*Genuine, trustworthy, of sound quality.*	*Copper plating on the bottom of a ship's hull protected the timbers from infestation, which had the added effect of increasing speed.*

Cranky	*Irritable, quick tempered.*	*A crank (the word might be from the Dutch 'krengd') was an unstable vessel, possibly due to badly loaded cargo, that would be hard to steer.*
Keel-hauling	*Being really told off/punished.*	*A sailor who suffered this punishment would be hauled, using ropes, from one side of the boat to the other, underneath (the keel).*
Knowing the ropes	*To know how a task should be done, understanding the routines.*	*With there being so many ropes on a sailing ship, it was a mark of a sailor's skills to be able to identify each one.*
A loose cannon	*Someone who is unpredictable or does their own thing.*	*A cannon which had come loose, being extremely heavy, could cause a lot of serious damage.*
A nipper	*Either a small child or a tool (a pair of) for cutting or gripping.*	*Nippers were small pieces of rope which enabled an anchor to be weighed and they were removed by small boys.*
A square meal	*A substantial meal which really fills you up.*	*When conditions allowed for the sailors to sit down and eat a good meal, they used square, wooden plates.*

Portsmouth Harbour

Idsworth

If you do decide to use the train from Petersfield, about half way through your journey, as you look through the window to your left, you may glimpse a small, isolated church on a hill, surrounded by fields and flowers. This is Idsworth Church. By car, travelling South from Chalton, you'll need to look out for a small gate marking the path up the hill.

This ancient church once overlooked a small village, now only visible from above when, in dry weather, marks show where buildings once stood. So, what happened to this village?

St Hubert's Church, hiding behind a hedge as you drive along can, conversely, be seen from way off

Black Death

In 1348 trading ships arriving in the Southwest, possibly at Bristol or Dorset, brought with them more than just valuable cargo. Yersinia pestis – so it is believed – crawled its way ashore, as rats – we have long supposed – made landfall, bringing the bacteria, along with the fleas that helped transfer it to its human victims. Historians and scientists still debate how the disease made its way across the globe: even fluffy little gerbils have been credited, so maybe Ratty was not to blame!

Over the previous couple of years the Black Death had oozed its way Northwards across Europe before breeching the barrier of the English Channel.

The population of England was ill-prepared. Thirteen forty-eight had been yet another summer of rain and ruined harvests. People up and down the land were suffering from malnutrition, and their resistance to infection was at a low ebb.

Similar in its consequences, and possibly even the same infection, it is all too easy to confuse this attack of pestilence which devastated the English population in the mid-

fourteenth century with "The Plague" during the reign of King Charles II. With higher literacy among the people, the later outbreak was better documented, including Samuel Pepys' diary and Daniel Defoe's 'Journal of the Plague Year'.

Fewer records remain of the devastation from 1348-1350. Thus it was that villages like the settlement at Idsworth could be erased from existence. Sometimes the majority of a village's population might have been eradicated in just a few days or weeks.

Sometimes, once the pestilence arrived, the other villagers would flee, abandoning the cluster of houses to time and the elements. Tragically, those evacuating one village might be already incubating the disease and would then contaminate a previously untouched community.

Lomer, a few miles further back along the South Downs Way, may have been abandoned for another reason: land enclosures, when landowners chose to keep sheep, requiring less man-power, which in consequence would displaced a population.

Mercilessly, the Black Death marched through the country. It is estimated that between twenty and forty percent of England's population were killed by the disease over a period of two years. This was about two million people. Sometimes, in the countryside, there were not enough survivors to bury the dead.

Recent examination of data estimates that in London the fatalities may have been as high as sixty percent of the inhabitants. It seems incredible that it could have been so contagious, but it is likely that the bacteria mutated from bubonic to pneumonic: air-borne – passed on by the coughing and sneezing of its victims to new hosts – a far quicker and more deadly means of transmission.

It is easy to think the contagion disappeared as quickly as it had arrived: less than a year after reaching our shores the number of cases peaked and within a few more weeks the tidal wave had gone. In fact, there were fresh outbreaks every few years for centuries, and because the young had not built up any immunity in previous outbreaks, these fresh outbreaks disproportionally seemed to target the young.

And if you think that bubonic plague is only to be found in history books – think again!

There are still small pockets of Yersinia pestis throughout the world. For example, in just one year there were sixty victims in Madagasca alone!

In this country there was an outbreak of the pneumonic variety in Suffolk at the beginning of the twentieth century. So, perhaps it's a good idea not to forget the rhyme: "Coughs and sneezes spread diseases".

In the fourteenth century, people had no idea how to protect themselves from this killer, so many strange methods were used to prevent catching it, from flagellation (self-inflicted whipping to show God you were sorry for your sins) to blaming those of a different religion and slaughtering them (we really have made progress over the last seven hundred or so years on that one), with a bit of aromatherapy thrown in for good measure (Mmm! Doesn't that lavender make you feel good?).

Once infected, it wasn't long before the casualty began to feel unwell. Large dark swellings – the buboes – bursting with bacteria, would begin to swell up. The victims were said to bark like dogs, so great was the agony. Death followed shortly afterwards. The pneumonic version spread more quickly, its incubation period was about half the time and it killed its victims just as rapidly. The good news was that there were no buboes with this variant.

In fact, epidemiologically, the disease was not very good at its job, which was to reproduce itself by infecting as many victims as possible. Why? Well, it killed people too quickly! The longer the 'target' was infected but feeling well, the more people who would also be infected! That's why the 'common cold' is so common.

As well as the loss of life, the consequences for England were the upheaval of the social structure...livestock and land were left unmanaged...wealth and trade...well, frankly, everything was in turmoil. As the government tried to maintain the old ways with new laws, the oppressed peasants rose up in anger. Which leads us to the Peasants' Revolt and Watt Tyler (or the Pedant's Revolt, as grammatically it should be 'Which Tyler?').

So, although no-one can be certain what happened to a congregation so long ago, their disappearance, leaving only a church, could well have been the result of this global disaster.

Now, I've wandered so far off track, I think that it's time to get back to the quiet little church – St Hubert's – at Idsworth.

High on a Hill was a Lonely...

This church, dedicated to St Hubert in the nineteenth century, was built just a few years before the Norman Invasion of 1066, during a time when many other churches were constructed (the churches at Corhampton and Chilcomb are of a similar period). These days, its location along with its simplicity – a largely white building with simple, plain glass windows – feels peaceful, a place for quiet contemplation.

Once cleansed of those wall paintings, the Puritans probably loved the simplicity of St Hubert's

However, in places there are flashes of colour on the walls indicating a much livelier environment in the past. These are the remnants of wall paintings which probably decorated the whole church in its heyday.

In an era when the populace was often illiterate (basic literacy did increase throughout

the mediaeval period) and the services were in Latin, these images brought the people closer to their God, telling the stories of the Bible, the lives of the saints and uplifting moral tales. There were versions of the Bible in English, but State control over the use of Latin in religious texts certainly became more authoritarian and controversial by the time of King Henry VIII.

Here at Idsworth there are more paintings, hidden for many years like those at Corhampton, which have been revealed. The quality of the work upon these walls is highly regarded by the experts in the field of art history.

A Close Shave...

(might have been a good idea with this story)

Now, one of the stories identified here is that of Jan of Beverley. Beverley is in Yorkshire, so it seems strange that the legend appears here. On the other hand, I got a Christmas card this year with a nativity scene in a thatched barn set in a snowy landscape (soooo Bethlehem, don't you think? It does occasionally snow there, but the thatched roof?), so maybe scene shifting is not so unusual, and the story was felt to have some moral purpose for the folk here in Hampshire.

So, here goes with the story of The Hairy Anchorite!

Jan ('John' with a Yorkshire accent or just to avoid confusion with another character called John) is weighed down by the comfortable life he has and so he goes off to live as a hermit, visited occasionally by his sister. Along comes the Devil and tells him his eternal salvation can only be secured if he commits one of three sins: drunkenness, the old favourite – sex, or murder.

He persuades his sister to bring the drink so he can follow instructions. Inebriated, he then rapes and buries her. So, that covers all three of the options! Isn't one of the Seven Deadly Sins 'greed'? If so, he isn't doing very well.

Now, truly feeling guilty, he nips off to the Pope in Rome, seeking absolution, but the

Pope says he's gone too far, advising him to seek the advice of John of Beverley (hence the need to avoid the confusion of Jan/John).

Past the wit of man to say where this strange tale come from

Jan sets his own punishment: to walk on all fours, eat grass, drink water and to remain speechless until a one-day-old baby tells him of God's forgiveness.

Well, seven long years pass until this happens (only seven years to find such a child?). He confesses his crimes to the Archbishop of Canterbury and then returns to the grave of his sister to unearth her and...well, I never...she is still alive and able to tell stories of her time in Paradise!

Jan and his sister go off together, happily praising God.

And When the Saints go Marching In...

Stories like this and images of the saints were, fortunately for us, preserved through the centuries of religious change.

The colours must have been wonderful and uplifting. And the saints must have been instantly recognisable, even to visitors to the parish, because, rather like footballers today, they had their own 'strip'. The teams on the huge TV showing a World Cup match in the pub are instantly recognisable: Brazil in the yellow and green, England in the white – this means that you can follow the game easily. So, Saint Peter with his keys to the gates of Heaven, in blue with gold, could be easily distinguished from Saint Matthew in red with blue or Saint Mark wearing red with green. The ordinary people could interpret the images around them as they prayed.

Bringing in the Decorators

It is unlikely the parishioners would have done the paintings themselves. More likely, it would have been a commission for a craftsman with a good reputation.

These days, I must confess, they look a lot of 'beige' to me: lots of browns and yellows but little sign of anything else. Well, age does none of us any favours, and such is the case here. Of the pigments used, the 'earth' colours – the ochres and siennas have survived the centuries. The brighter, and often more expensive (frequently imported), pigments have not. The minerals would have undergone various combinations of grinding, filtration and heating to produce a wide range of pigments.

Fresco...Secco...Every Little Helps!

So, how is it done?

First, take one wall. Plaster it. Okay, let's slow up a bit. Any modern builder will know about the first coats, the brown and scratch ones, and so it is with lime plaster. This base is called the arriccio. It has to dry before the intonaco, the fine top-coat is applied.

For the purpose of a wall-painting, the plaster is applied an area at a time, and a stylus is used to mark the design. At this stage no fancy mixing of paint is required. It is just pigment and water. This needs to be done fairly quickly, before the plaster undergoes chemical changes (partial carbonisation) as it dries.

At this stage it is what is called a fresco. Now, in warm Mediterranean countries, this would be an hour or so, whereas the high humidity in England means that work doesn't need to be so rushed.

The artist then changes the medium, mixing in some more lime and casein (a protein in milk) to enable work to continue, and the extra time allowed for some detail.

Once the plaster has dried, time is no longer the master and the artist has time to add the finishing touches. This technique is called secco. This time the pigment is mixed with egg yolk (tempera): that's the paint used by artists on board or canvas before the invention of oil paints.

There you have it: a wall painting!

Lift up (your) eyes unto the hills...and the Lord

mis-quote of Psalm 121

Despite the Mediaeval wall paintings around you, take time to sit down in a pew near the back of the nave and look up.

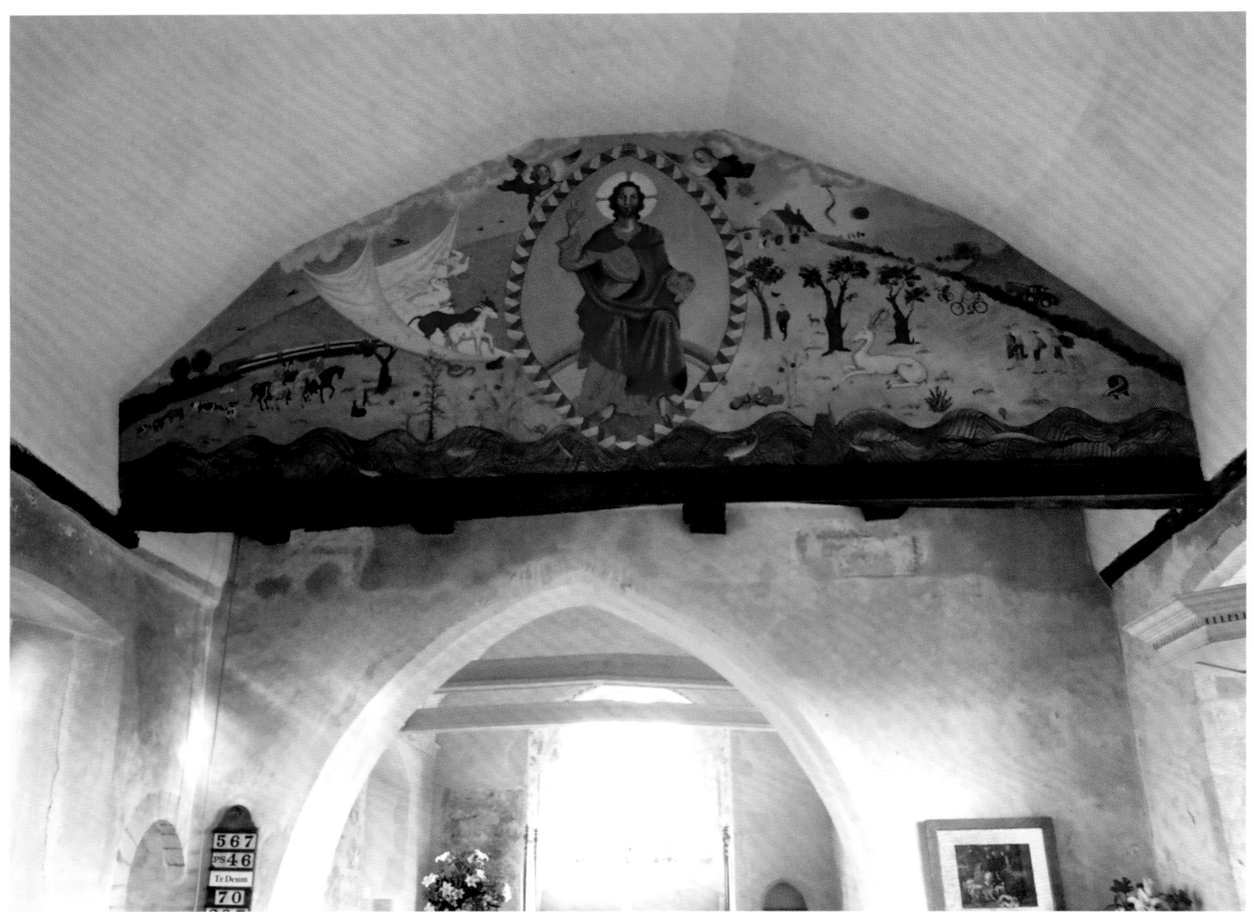

The Millennium Fresco

A revelation indeed! Yes: a modern wall painting – from the year 2000 – a riot of colour, providing a glimpse of what an attendance at a service must have been like half a millennia ago, when such opulence would have been all around the congregation.

Centrally placed is Christ, surrounded by images of modern times at Idsworth. In the painted hills surrounding Him are animals, plants, people and objects around at the time of its creation. There is a wedding party; vehicles including a tractor and a helicopter; a range of flowers, harebells and poppies among them; farm and wild animals – including the snail, so loved by gardeners – and, most important for those walking the South Downs Way: rucksack-bearing hikers!

The artist was Fleur Kelly, an experienced artist in the field (literally so at St

Hubert's). This reflects life in the middle ages, when the paintings would have been executed by itinerant experts, who would have been highly skilled.

The installation of this modern work has its lovers who feel that a work celebrating Christ in the new Millennium, using traditional techniques is a worthy addition, and its detractors for whom this modern take on the traditional is inappropriately situated. Some people love it and others loathe it, but it does stimulate conversation.

Petersfield

Approaching Petersfield, along the A3, a large brown sign pointing you towards the town announces boldly that it is an 'historic market' one. Well, I saw no indication of an 'historic market', whatever that might be (mediaeval merchants selling bolts of silks, taffetas and woollen fabrics, tools, beasts of the field and the labourers to care for them?). However, there is a weekly market in the town square selling fruit, veg, and various items of clothing. I bought a cardigan there, and very nice it was too.

Character cottages abound in Petersfield

As for the historic bit, there is a local museum and a gallery – with the delightful name Flora Twort – and aged buildings of various eras. Attractive and charming, they give the town a warm character. However, there are no castles, National Trust mansions serving cream teas en route to the gift shop, or public buildings to be gasped at for their antiquity or grandeur. Even English Heritage's annual Open Days do not seem to have encouraged the good townsfolk of Petersfield to have flung open their front doors in welcome! Actually, in Hampshire it is Gosport which seems to have leapt into the spirit of the occasion with both feet.

Of course, this town's location does make it a good pit-stop on the journey to and from Portsmouth, and in the days before the motor car, such a stop off would be a much needed break for travellers.

Since the coming of the railway, the town has been blessed with a station, allowing for the easy transporting of goods and produce to and from London, like other towns on the line. It has given Petersfield a chance to burgeon since Victorian times. These days, it is where travellers can pause mid chapter, look out through the window, glance at their watches to calculate how long it will be until they reach their destination and then settle down again. Meanwhile, others barely notice as they stare zombie-like at mobile technology, perhaps announcing to their fellow travellers that they are on the train.

However, that railway means that Petersfield has continued to grow into what can only be described as a fairly prosperous town, giving a good living to local estate agents.

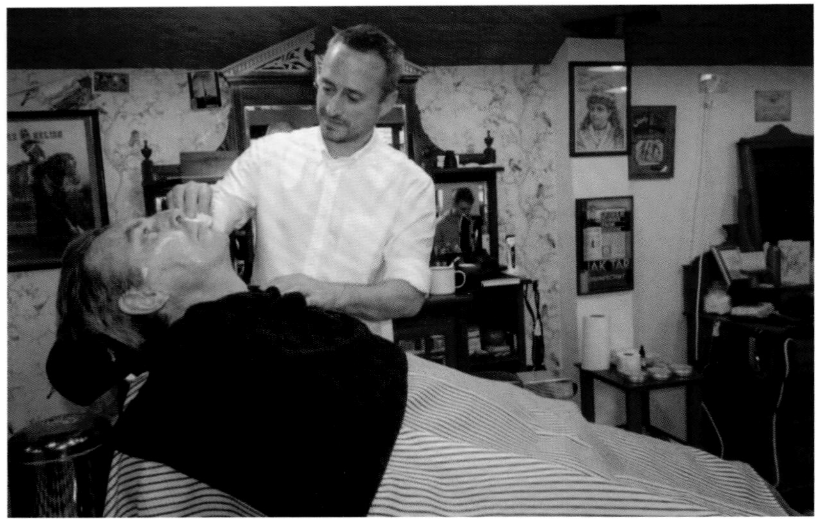

Among the independent shops is Sweeny Plod's. And what else would you call a traditional barber's owned by a former policeman?

As well as the market, there is a good range of shops, many from the ubiquitous chains, but also quite a few independent ones, giving residents and visitors the opportunity for some retail therapy.

The town appears to invite shoppers. There is plenty of car parking and – happily – a good supply of public conveniences. However, for a town which encourages shoppers, these well-maintained loos don't seem to have been provisioned with hooks for handbags and carrier bags! Not very convenient! Perhaps this sums up my ambivalence about Petersfield – there's a lot on the surface.

Around the market square

Nonetheless, it is a useful town with its railway station and quite a few places to stay for those doing a section of the South Downs Way, and also for the more enduring hiker to stock up on supplies. In the evenings there are plenty of pubs and restaurants to while away a few hours and to stoke up the energy reserves for any walking the following day.

However, there is no cinema or theatre to liven up the evening, which is surprising for a town of this size, as even considerably smaller communities can draw in large audiences for their occasional film-nights. It is worth stating that local groups do organise events, if you are lucky enough for your visit to coincide.

Perhaps this explains one aspect of the town that did surprise me: there are two dedicated book shops – in addition to the shelves in charity shops, second hand bookstores and newsagents. For a population of approximately 15,000, this means one shop for every 7,500 people.

An internet search of a dozen randomly selected towns and cities in England showed this to be quite remarkable! In many towns there are at least ten times the number of people per shop (the worst I found was 274,000 per shop). In my modest survey, Petersfield was only beaten by Keswick, its one bookshop serving a population of about 5,000 – oh, and that town also has a fantastic theatre.

So, perhaps Petersfield's literate crowd of bibliophiles don't have time for other amusements.

If you are staying over in Petersfield and you need a stroll to work up an appetite before your repast, there is a 'village pond': an understatement for both words. Petersfield is no village and the pond is more like a lake, at twenty-two acres. The Heath's huge expanse is a countryside treat, as a place for leisure and a wildlife reserve.

Petersfield Pond: from marsh to marvellous

Amazingly, it is not a work of nature. Nearly three centuries ago, in 1741, locals with grazing rights were frustrated by a marshy area which was unusable and they had also seen the demise of grazing animals which had strayed into these dangerous pastures, sinking so deeply into the mire they would expire. These people banded together to dig deep into the landscape, creating this wonderful feature in the process, which allowed the surrounding water to drain into it and for the fields to dry out.

So, there is some history here, even if it is not in ancient markets and venerable buildings for tourists to enter and admire. Petersfield is far too modern for these.

For centuries it was exactly what the name suggests – Saint Peter's field – the land around St Peter's Church in the parish of Buriton. As time went by, helped by the wool trade, houses (some of which are still there) trades and businesses sprung up around it. But it was not until as recently as 1886 that it became a town in its own right.

Ding Dong Merrily...

And while we're about it, the church itself, a Grade 1 listed building, is early Norman and may have been founded by Queen Matilda, the wife of William the Conqueror. Its broad rounded arches, a feature which usually creates solidity, and with it gloom, are here bathed in light and cheerfulness. Later changes have been made, including the addition of some Perpendicular Gothic windows in the fifteenth century, which may account for the freshness.

Sunday Morning Worship at St Peter's Church

Let's not, however, think that everything has always been sweetness and light, humanity and goodwill with religion in this location.

At the end of the eighteenth century, the Church of England did not think highly of the Nonconformists, and disputes were not uncommon. Petersfield's Congregational Church was honoured to have a preacher, Richard Densham, who could draw in large crowds.

St Peter's overlooking the market square

Densham was the ordained minister appointed in 1799 who attracted large audiences, and he had the energy to spread his beneficence widely. For example, his itinerary for the second day of August in 1800 started at Harting with ninety listeners. At eleven o'clock he addressed a crowd at Petersfield, moving on to East Meon by two o'clock with an encore two hours later. His evening at Rogate attracted five hundred followers. The Vicar at Petersfield must have been more than just disgruntled.

The next morning, the Reverend Densham was on his way to Haslemere for another day of spreading the gospel when he was thrown from his gig – a light, two-wheeled carriage – killing him.

At his funeral in Petersfield, a few days later, the town's church rang its bells so loudly and continuously, it drowned out the service for the late lamented non-conformist preacher! Revenge is sweet: ding dong!

The Physic Garden, just off the High Street. A good place for some peace and quiet ... and your picnic?

Buriton

A Bit of Chalk and Talk!

In a school I recently visited, underneath the projector screen (which is damned to failure during power cuts and IT disasters) was a white board (upon which out-of-control pens slither for just a few words before the ink runs dry), and underneath that was trapped the beloved blackboard upon which – long ago – neat script would be attained with that wonderful stuff called chalk!

For some of us, that is a never-fading memory: chalk, along with a collection of words and phrases embedded into our language: 'as white as chalk', 'chalk and cheese', 'not by a long chalk', 'slaking your thirst'...and so on.

Chalk is, however, used in many other ways. You can chalk up its uses including on the end of a snooker cue, helping gymnasts grab the bar, stone for building and as a medium for artists. Once converted into lime, it fertilises fields, is used in manufacturing and it is a component in cement and plaster.

In its various forms, it has been used by mankind for millennia. It stores water, filters water, contains flints for tools and weapons. It was those flint fragments remaining in the sticks of chalk which would make that cringing squeak when your teacher wrote on the blackboard.

So, apart from white stuff, what is it? Chalk is part of the limestone group of rocks. It was formed in tropical seas over 130 million years ago, in the Cretaceous period. And Cretaceous is simply from the Latin word 'creta' meaning 'chalk'. So it would be far easier if the era was known as 'the chalk period'!

Floating in a warm ancient sea was plankton, along with fish and shellfish. When the various organisms died, the skeletons sank to the bottom and formed a sludgy layer. The warmth, along with the pressure of yet more stuff landing on top, squashed it into chalk. And there you have it! Chalk!

As tectonic plates deep beneath us pushed and shoved around, lumps and bumps of rock stuck out above the surface, including those little hills we call the Alps, as well as the South and North Downs. You may not believe it as you stroll along the South Downs Way but, world-wide, chalk is quite rare: chalk cliffs and ridges are generally only to be found in Northern Europe. And those earth tremors are still pushing them around.

The layering of chalk, although this example is from near to Meon Springs

So, the landscape of the Downs is quite rare and has flowers on the chalky soil that have adapted themselves to this environment, including the round headed rampion and the pasqueflower. Butterflies flutter delicately amongst them, including the Adonis blue and the Gatekeeper.

Man, however, has a habit of using nature's resources, so he has chipped at, dug out, crushed and burned the chalk for his own advantage. For these reasons, quarry workings and lime kilns have been an industrial use of the landscape for centuries.

With the Industrial Revolution, large-scale workings have scarred the landscape, as has happened here at Buriton.

From the mid-nineteenth century, this area – just South of Buriton – was a hive of industrial activity, with quarries, kilns and its own railway line shunting the chalk around the site, and onwards to a link with the main London to Portsmouth railway line.

The chalk was dug out and then chugged down the hill to the kilns. You can still see evidence of the railway lines around the place. It was even better than the high-speed lines of today: only using gravity and with a man standing at the back of the truck, they'd reach speeds of fifty or sixty miles an hour! Leaves on the line? No problem! However, to get the trucks to the top again, they needed horsepower.

The detritus from its industrial past – one of the rail-trucks

Right, back to the chalk. In the kilns it was heated so that a chemical change ensued, converting the calcium carbonate (chalk) into calcium oxide (quicklime).

Once cooled, it is not stable. Rather like a teenager in school uniform waiting for the first chance to get back into their 'own' clothes, the quicklime is desperate to absorb the carbon dioxide (which was burnt off in the kiln) and turn itself back into chalk.

Although at this stage it has industrial uses, one being the making of cement, it is quite dangerous. For example, King Henry III used it in a sea battle: the quicklime was wafted towards the French enemy, blinding them!

So, the chalk has been changed into quicklime but it can then be changed again into

calcium hydroxide, otherwise known as slaked lime. By adding water (slaking it) it can be used for loads of things from water purification and lime plaster to perming your hair!

Lime plaster is the stuff that any DIY-er will know from that lovely pink finishing plaster which makes the freshly mixed goo so wonderfully warm. And, as this DIY-er knows, is extremely dangerous and painful if you get a dollop in the eye. The A & E department at your local hospital will rush you to the front of the queue.

Buriton chalk pit kiln (thanks to Buriton History Society for image)

But back to Buriton! All good things come to an end, and eventually the quarrying ceased in the 1930s. Its demise must have resulted in job loses, but with another war on the horizon there were plenty of new opportunities.

The Second World War gave the site a new lease of life as an area where mines could be safely defused by the Royal Navy. Up to 150 at a time might be at the site!

Somewhere in the area are the remnants of a gigantic x-ray machine, used by the military to examine inside the ammo for any boobytraps intended to trigger explosions during the process. Once the experts knew what they were dealing with, they would steam out the explosives and, at the same time, gather information about new enemy mines.

Peace brought with it a few years for the site as the home of a small business before its abandonment in the mid-1970s.

Once deserted, nature encroached and has reclaimed its territory. The way-marker here for the Shipwrights' Way is a Cheese Snail. It's a good job that the sculpture is so large and visible, as the real thing – a protected creature – is no bigger than a fingernail, and hides itself away discretely under decaying woodland.

The Cheese Snail way-marker: it's a good job snails are not really this big – imagine the damage to your hostas!

Now, anyone walking along the South Downs Way can pause and enjoy the Nature Reserve here at Buriton. At the top, close by the car-park, is a delightful pond (Man has been at it again here, restoring it from the industrial days) and behind that are woodland footpaths meandering through the old quarry, which take you down to the village, and a pub lunch gives you the strength to scamper back up the hill later in the day to resume your walk.

The Pedants' Revolt

The casual misuse of English in our writing is a crime which many of us have to own up to. Teachers of English must, therefore, either cuss or applaud Robert Lowth, who spent his childhood here in Buriton in the early eighteenth century.

Perhaps either of these responses is to misjudge him!

The son of the vicar, he grew up here and went on to achieve respect throughout the English speaking world for his academic work.

Schooled at Winchester, he moved on to study at Oxford. Having taken orders in the Anglican Church, it was a post at Ovington in Hampshire that he went on to.

Robert Lowth's home in Buriton

From whence he departed, upon being appointed Oxford Professor of Poetry.

Romance beckoned, and he resigned this post when he married.

His first acclaimed writing was his treatise on Hebrew religious poetry.

Initially, I thought Robert Lowth to be as dry as ditchwater or as dull as dust, until I read that his most important writing was – as far as me and you are concerned – his

'A Short Introduction to English Grammar' (1762), written for his son, Thomas. This puts him in the same league as A A Milne and Kenneth Grahame, who also penned works for their own children. His intention was to aid his son's learning of the rules guiding written English, but his advice was taken as the gospel truth by those requiring rules on how to achieve perfect writing.

Pond near the gates of the house

We all break these rules; either by error, or a lack of knowledge or deliberately (as an affectation of style or to make a point). Teachers, however, have ever since been burdened by the pedantic enforcement of Lowth's advice. Yes, it is pleasant to have a framework and an answer to the perennial question "Why?". However, the burdensome marking that has ensued should be a warning to the young and impressionable considering entering the profession that it's not a job for those who like a social life to go into!

So, what are these rules? Most famously, there is the one about not ending a sentence with a preposition (Winston Churchill's response was "Up with this I will not put!").

Then there is the Star Trek conundrum of the split infinitive: should we say "to boldly go" or (correctly) "to go boldly"?

Of the former of these strictures, Lowth did actually state that such a rule was for "solemn and elevated writing" and was not essential for everyday communications. However, the Victorian pedants took his advice as an immutable rule, and it has been set in grammatical stone hereafter.

Strangely, it was Lowth who outlawed the phrase "you was" which had been regarded as perfectly good English prior to his writing.

I suppose that we all have our favourite rules. I don't (however) think that I can blame Lowth for my twitchiness when I see misplaced apostrophes, but it is his dictat that has steam emitting from my ears when seeing or hearing "different to" (rather than "different from") and two negatives making a positive (as in "I ain't not guilty, me Lord.". He was (I understand) also unhappy (I can't imagine why) about the use of parenthesis (brackets to me and you)!

As he had written his book as helpful advice, not as didactic monoliths but to help his son with his school-work (and I bet that most of us have at some time helped with the homework), he must have (no – I don't think that this is one of his rules: it is just lexicographically insane to write "must of") turned in his grave as the Victorians adopted his humble book as the bible of good writing.

And now (because I've finished I deserve to definitely have a break), I'm going to happily switch the kettle on.

Grammar Knows Best!

I have a feeling that Robert Lowth is turning in his grave about apostrophes. Certainly, it has caused me a great deal of consternation with the names of footpaths as I have plodded my way through this book. At some points I have really been stomping: has no-one made a decision about apostrophes?

Earlier I wrote about the Monarchs Way, the Pilgrims Way, the St Swithuns Way, the Wayfarers Walk and the Shipwrights Way, as well as – of course – the South Downs Way (forgive me for the lack of apostrophes here). However, I have seen each of these routes variously written without apostrophes, with apostrophes before the s and with apostrophes after the s.

Sadly, I fear, this is an aspect where people are totally whimsical. For several months I have tried to get someone at Hampshire County Council to pronounce on the matter, to no avail (ignorance or can't be bothered: who knows?). I've tried the South Downs Way National Park, which sent a reply that has been helpful, although in some cases has settled for the old maxim "when in doubt, leave it out"!

So, for the sake of Mr Lowth, I have decided to make my own pronouncement!

Now, as far as I am aware there has only ever been one Saint Swithun (without looking through a complete hagiography, I cannot be sure, but I'll take a guess), so the Way must be dedicated to him. Therefore the apostrophe must be between the n and the s. Likewise, the Monarch referred to is one particular Charles Stuart, so once more the apostrophe should be before the s. Most people seem to be able to cope with these two, so I'm not too worried.

After the basics, things have become more complicated. In Mediaeval times there were a great many pilgrims who took time off work to respect Holy Days, so we need the apostrophe after the s of the Pilgrims' Way.

Disappointingly, even a web-site from Canterbury Cathedral can't get this right. You'd

think that they would know better. Strangely, the Pilgrims' Trail, leading to Winchester from Normandy seems not to have a problem!

Likewise, at the eastern end of the county, the apostrophe should follow the s as there were many shipwrights needed to build each vessel. However, if they were ever there, the apostrophes seem to have been chiselled out altogether, as I can't find any reference to the path that has one in place!

After all the effort of creating a footpath for wayfarers, I hope that the route is used with some frequency, resulting in more than one wayfarer, so I am declaring that this footpath also deserves its apostrophe to be placed after the s: the Wayfarers' Walk. The County Council chooses not to use one, as do several other bodies. This must be just 'can't be bovvered', as the council couldn't even bother to get back to me on this point! For goodness sake! This is Robert Lowth's birthplace!

At this point I am so exhausted, I am giving in to modern laziness regarding this lovely punctuation mark and leaving it out altogether with the South Downs Way.

So: I am declaring: we have the St Swithun's Way, the Monarch's Way, the Pilgrims' Way, the Wayfarers' Walk, the Shipwrights' Way and the South Downs Way!

Blow Winds, and Crack Your Cheeks!

King Lear; Wm. Shakespeare

Overlooking the village pond in Buriton is St Mary's Church. A visit there will give you the chance to see the West window, a seventeenth century memorial to John Goodyer and his wife, whose remains rest in the churchyard.

'Who?' you may ask. Well, until the last fifty years or so, his name and work had fallen into the black hole of obscurity. A botanist, born during the reign of Queen Elizabeth I, he seems to have spent his whole life in Hampshire, living at Droxford and then in Petersfield, which at the time was an outlying area of the parish of Buriton.

John Goodyer is buried here with his wife at St Mary's Church, which overlooks the pond. There is a memorial window to him inside.

He lived through the turbulent times of the English Civil War, an era when the scientific study of plant-life was taking root. He was a contemporary of the Tradescant family, who were among those who travelled the known world, bringing back exotic plant specimens.

In an age when it was fashionable to collect and grow unusual plants, John Goodyer added many plants to the panoply of British flora, and made detailed observations of many favourites.

For a man who was so highly regarded in his time (at the height of the Civil War, in 1643, the Royalist commander Ralph Hopton instructed his men "to defend and protect John Goodyer, his house, family, servants and estates!") it is sad how he was then forgotten until his papers, kept at Magdalen College Oxford, were unearthed comparatively recently.

Remarkably, botany was not his job – he was an estate manager at Mapledurham House, which used to be nearby. He was, I suppose, what we might these days call a 'hobbyist': someone whose true talent was also his leisure activity.

He lived into his seventies, a good age for the seventeenth century, and following his death, shortly after that of his wife, he was buried near to her at St Mary's Church.

With no children, he left land and property in his will to enable a charity to provide assistance to the needy: primarily for the education and training of children, and this charity is still operational in the twenty first century.

He is also highly regarded for two particular aspects of his botanical work. Firstly, he has a genus of orchid named after him: orchid Goodyera.

It is in Petersfield where you will find Goodyer's house

Secondly, he introduced a vegetable to this country, called the Jerusalem Artichoke. Confusingly, it is not an artichoke. Oh, and it's not from Jerusalem. The Jerusalem bit is a corruption of the name 'girasole', which is the Italian for sunflower, and indeed it is a member of the sunflower family. The flavour is supposed to be a bit artichokey (the globe artichoke), so that accounts for the second part of the name.

It is not the flowers, seeds nor foliage that is eaten, but the tubers, the swollen roots – like potatoes. They are often used similarly to potatoes in the kitchen too. More knobbly than the noble spud, its flavour has been described as 'nutty', 'garlicky' and 'mushroomy' among others. It is quite sweet, but it is supposed to be fairly healthy – full of something called inulin – and a good source for vitamins and minerals.

Ideal for the garden and kitchen? Well, yes. Except it is rather invasive in the garden. And it has a well-deserved terrible reputation for causing flatulence.

And now... the end is here!

After all, tomorrow is another day!

<u>Gone with the Wind</u>; Margaret Mitchell

Most books end with something memorable. Unfortunately, this book ends on rather an anti-climax! Although I did not expect the Massed Bands of the Royal Marines to wave me over the border into West Sussex with a cheery tune, something would have been nice: a sign post, for example.

However, there is nothing. Wandering back and forth with my OS Map, I waylaid a group of passing cyclists (is there a collective noun? A chain? A hub? – motorists probably have their own expletives) to ask for their advice. Charming as they were, after long perusal of the map and much debate, we were none the wiser.

The ash tree that seems to be at the border between Hampshire and West Sussex

Wandering up-hill from Sunwood Farm, I had passed through the point where a grey 'dot and dash' line crosses the South Downs Way on the map, but didn't even notice! I had passed a large, lonely ash tree, just beyond which the farm owners believe the boundary to be.

Being rather short, and the hedges rather tall, I didn't even have a view!

Turning back to take the final look at Hampshire before wandering on, in my mind's eye I saw a jolly pig waving at me from where the county boundary should be, with a sign quoting Hilaire Belloc's comment upon the county: "Hampshire Hic Porci - here be pigs". Why he made it I don't know, but it is a cheery picture to have in my mind.

Moving on into West Sussex, perhaps two very different sources for literary quotations should be given (in one case the beauty of the language is in stark contrast to the content of the source):

> *"Then starting home, he walked toward the trees, and under them, leaving behind him the big sky, the whisper of wind voices in the wind-bent wheat."*
>
> In Cold Blood; Truman Capote

and

> *"So they went off together. But wherever they go, and whatever happens to them on the way, in that enchanted place on the top of the Forest a little boy and his Bear will always be playing."*
>
> The House at Pooh Corner; A A Milne

Looking back across the Hampshire landscape

Look out for future books in the series

For more information contact:

redbakpublishing.co.uk